ON STAGE

ON STAGE

How to Put on a Play

Patricia
Sternberg

Julian Messner New York

Manufactured in the United States of America
Design by Irving Perkins Associates
Photos by Jane Hoffer
Library of Congress Cataloging in Publication Data

Sternberg, Patricia.
  On stage.

  Bibliography: p.
  Includes index.
  Summary: Discusses the three elements necessary
for putting on a production: cast, play, and audience.
Also includes tips on acting and writing one's own
play.
  1. Amateur theater—Juvenile literature.
[1. Theater—Production and direction] I. Title.
PN3155.S68   1982   792'.0222   82-60651
ISBN 0-671-45246-0

For my favorite young players, David, Ruth, and Anne

ACKNOWLEDGMENT

The author gratefully acknowledges the help of the following people: Dolly Beechman, colleague and dear friend, for her advice and assistance with this book and her theatre experiences shared with me; Julie and Sheldon Thompson, for giving me those first wondrous and joyful theatre experiences; and William Talbot of Samuel French, Inc., for his assistance.

CONTENTS

Putting on a play takes enthusiasm, hard work, and cooperation among many people.

Chapter 1

The Play's the Thing

So you want to put on a play? Well, you're not alone. Nearly everyone has that urge sooner or later. Almost all of us think about it—and lots of people try it.

"I never worked so hard or had so much fun before in my whole life." "You'd never guess how many hours we had to rehearse it!" These comments are frequently heard after a successful play performance.

Few activities create the bond of camaraderie or promote the self-discipline and hard work it takes to put on a play. There aren't many moments more exhilarating than the sound of applause from an appreciative audience.

There must be something very special about performing a play. People have been putting on plays for as long as they have been recording history.

Shakespeare said:

All the world's a stage,
And all the men and women merely players;

> They have their exits and their entrances,
> And one man in his time plays many parts . . .
>> *As You Like It*
>> ACT II, SCENE 7, LINE 140

Those of us who have put on a play know how much time and effort it takes. If you want to try a play for the first time, be forewarned—it's hard work! It's also well worth the effort.

But if you're still determined (and that's the first step) and like a challenge, here are some simple *Do's* and *Don'ts* to help you get started.

DO
- Plan your production carefully.
- Pick a group of people who can cooperate with each other.
- Give yourself enough time to rehearse the performance adequately.
- Keep it simple.
- Keep it fun.

DON'T
- Try to compete with Broadway.
- Pick a play you can't cast.
- Try to perform a play with too little rehearsal time.
- Use complicated sets, props, or costumes.
- Try to force your ideas on others.

Now that you have considered some preliminary *Do's* and *Don'ts,* where do you begin? What do you do first? Let's begin with the three elements necessary for putting on a production: the cast (or performers), the play, and the audience.

THE CAST

Although there are no hard and fast rules of what to do first, you may want to ask yourself the following questions before you proceed.

Who will be the performers in the play? Will they be a group of friends, a club group, or a class in school? Will a group of strangers come together to do the play?

You will want to consider the size of your group also. How many people will be involved? If there are twelve people in your group, you won't want to choose a play like *The Gin Game*. (It has only two characters.) On the other hand, if you have six friends who want to put on a play, don't choose *Nicholas Nickleby*. (Forty-two actors play over 150 parts.)

Let us say you have decided to do a play with a club group. How many people will be involved? Remember, not everyone will want to act. There are some people who would rather work behind stage than on it. And, that's fine! When you put on a play, there are plenty of jobs in addition to acting.

THE PLAY

The next question to ask is: Where will you put on your play?

Certain plays lend themselves to certain kinds of staging. Some plays can be done more easily in one place than another. That's why your facilities limit your choice of a play.

Don't let yourself be fooled by the idea that you must

have a theater or even an auditorium to do a play. Insisting on a stage is one of the biggest mistakes beginners can make. There are dozens of plays that can be put on just as well in the center of a large room with little or no scenery. There are plays that can be done successfully in a classroom.

Select a play that can be produced easily in the space you have available. If you use a standard auditorium with a curtain and a raised stage at one end, you are doing *proscenium* staging. When you do your play in the center of a large open space, it is called *arena* staging or theater in the round.

Now ask yourself a vital question: What play will you do?

There are as many different kinds of plays as there are people. You can find a play dealing with every subject imaginable. There are plays for specific purposes like holidays, fire prevention, or the Red Cross blood drive. There are plays with outlandish characters that provide laughs galore. And there are plays that bring tears and thoughtful memories for years to come.

Before you select your play, think about the group who will work on it. Every good director chooses a play that he or she knows can be cast with the available talent.

If you have three girls in your group who want to act, select a play like *Vanities*, which has three female characters in it. If you have a very strong actor or actress, you may want to choose a play with a starring role. (This type of play is primarily dependent on one person.)

Most of the time when you begin, you don't know the ability of your performers unless you've seen them in a play before. In that case, give yourself some insurance. Choose a play that has several roles of similar length. That kind of play is an *ensemble* piece. It offers more roles for more people than the star vehicle does.

There's an old saying in the theater: "There are no small parts—only small actors." That means that every role in a play is equally important to the whole production. And it is true. You will soon find out that a play, like any team effort, is just as strong as its weakest link. At some moment during the course of the play, the production is dependent on each individual actor. Each actor must play his role to the best of his ability as a part of the whole production.

Imagine that you've decided to do an ensemble play for your first experience. Are there any particular plays that are easier than others? Some plays are called "actor proof." That means that the play itself is so good that almost any actors can play it successfully.

Many mysteries are "actor proof." In order to offer a variety of suspects, there are usually a lot of interesting and distinctive characters of about the same length. Some comedies and some melodramas fit into this category also.

Keep in mind that your play should be fun to do. Make sure your group is enthusiastic about the project. Don't be fooled into thinking only comedy can be fun. There are all kinds of plays that promote this spirit of fun and camaraderie among the players.

Let's briefly consider the cost of putting on a play.

Even though you keep your production elements down to a minimum, there are some expenses that crop up. Request funds from your club treasury or ask for contributions from your group, so that the financial burden doesn't fall on one person. When everyone shares part of the cost, no one person has to get stuck. Be prepared for such expenses as copies of scripts, posters, tickets, and programs. Some plays require royalty payments. (There will be more about that later.) If you want to keep costs down to an absolute minimum, find people who will contribute time and materials for each of the above items.

If you decide to do a costume show or one with an unusual set or complicated props, you will need a fairly large budget. Chapter 4 goes into detail about budgets for each type of play. For now, remember that some money or volunteer time and materials will be necessary for every play.

Another thing to consider in your play selection is how much time you have to work on the show. It takes twice as much time to put on a full-length play as it does to put on a one-act play. And it takes two or three times the amount of time to put on a musical as it does to put on a straight play.

Suppose you decide to put on a play for your last club meeting of the term. That gives you a date to shoot for, and it tells you how much time you have for rehearsals. Let's say you have one month for rehearsals. (Broadway actors rehearse eight hours a day for three weeks and sometimes longer. That doesn't count the outside time they spend on their own, learning lines and creating their characters.)

You might decide to choose a one-act play for your first venture. Most people prefer to see a simple thing done well rather than a sloppy, over-ambitious undertaking that disappoints the actors as well as the audience. You can always work your way up to a more difficult production after you have mastered the simple ones. Remember that old saying: "Nothing succeeds like success."

If your first production is a success, you and your friends will be eager to put on more plays.

If you have the time, you can try a full-length play.

Perhaps you are part of a drama club that plans to work together for some time. In that case, you can think in long-range terms. You can spend more time on actor preparation. You may want to try to write your own play. (See Chapter 10.)

You have many points to consider when you make your final play selection. Chapters 4 and 5 offer detailed advice to help with your final decision.

THE AUDIENCE

Now you're ready to consider the last of the three elements necessary for putting on a play—the audience.

Who is your audience? Will you be performing this play for your family and friends? Will you sell tickets? Is it a fund-raiser for your group?

If you charge admission to the play, you have an additional responsibility to give your audience a quality product. The ideal, of course, is to enjoy the process of creating your performance while still offering a satisfying product to the audience.

If you think this sounds difficult, you're right! There's nothing more challenging than putting on a good play while enjoying the preparation at the same time.

I once heard a director refuse to sell tickets to the performance of a play. "It's not ready yet," she said, and offered free admission during the first week of the run until she felt the production was worth the price of a ticket. She said, "*Professional* is an attitude. It has nothing to do with whether anyone is paid or not. It means doing your very best work and giving your all to the effort."

Later on in this book, you will get more advice for solving specific problems that may occur during the course of your production. Review your answers to these four questions, and you are ready to begin play production.

- Who are the performers?
- Where will you perform the play?
- What play will you do?
- Who is your audience?

Once these decisions are made, you're on your way toward making it possible to hear that phrase which sends a shiver of excitement up everyone's spine. . . . "Curtain going up!"

2

Getting Organized

Which comes first? The chicken or the egg? That's the old question. But in our case, the question might be: The play or the people? Do you get your people together first and then pick a play? Or do you pick a play and then get the people? Actually, either way can work equally well. But you must decide which way to work.

If you already have a group of people in school or in your club who want to put on a play, then the decision is made for you. You must find a play with enough roles and production jobs to keep everyone happy. Since you know the people who will be involved, your selection of a play is easier than if you had to pick a play for an unknown group.

Most directors either know some of the people who will be acting in the play, or they are careful to choose a play with an ensemble cast. That means the play is not dependent on any one person. If there are six people in your club, you will want a play with six good parts.

One director said, "Any director who picks a play he can't cast is no director at all."

All right! You have selected your play. (For more about play selection, see Chapters 4 and 5.)

Now what? Besides the actors, what are the other jobs involved in putting on a play? You'll be surprised at how many other things you'll learn to do. One teenage actor fixes all of his mother's broken lamps since he learned about stage lighting.

In most amateur theaters, the actors also do the production jobs. Keep your job assignments as simple as possible to start.

ORGANIZATION

The following table of organization will be helpful for you to remember:

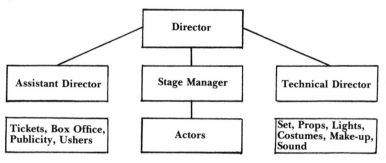

You can develop your own production organization so that it will work for your particular group.

THE STAGE MANAGER

In addition to the director, another essential job is that of the stage manager. The actors can double on other jobs, but the stage manager can do only one job.

Select your stage manager as carefully as you select your best friend. He or she must be someone you can trust, a person who is dependable and works hard and well with others. At least, try to find someone who comes close to that ideal description. Once the curtain goes up on opening night, the stage manager runs the show.

The various crews who work backstage during the performance are responsible to the stage manager. With so many people backstage, how do you keep them quiet? That's another job for the stage manager. If there's one thing that upsets every director, it's noise backstage.

A high-school director said, "I can always find actors. What I need is a good stage manager."

The stage manager runs the show during a performance. He or she gives cues for sound, lights, etc. (Some famous people started out as stage managers. The actor Henry Fonda is one.)

BLOCKING

The stage manager or S.M. prepares the prompt book. This book includes all the *blocking* and *business*. (Blocking designates where the actors move on the stage. Business indicates what they do, e.g., pick up a dish, straighten a picture, take off a shoe.) Light cues, sound cues, and important prop cues are also noted in the prompt book.

A prompt book is made up from the script. If it is a typed script on regular typing paper, the blocking is written in the margins. If it is a printed script from a play publisher, each page is pasted separately on a single piece of looseleaf paper in a notebook. A square the size of the

take nurse's
hands, pull
her DSC

Hast thou met with him? Send thy man away.
 Nurse. Peter, stay at the gate.   [*Exit Peter.*]
 Juliet. Now good sweet Nurse—O Lord, why look'st
    thou sad?
Though news be sad, yet tell them merrily;
If good, thou sham'st the music of sweet news
By playing it to me with so sour a face.
 Nurse. I am aweary, give me leave awhile.
Fie, how my bones ache! what a jaunce have I!
 Juliet. I would thou hadst my bones and I thy news.
Nay come, I pray thee, speak! Good, good Nurse,
    speak!
 Nurse. Jesu, what haste! can you not stay awhile?
Do you not see that I am out of breath?
 Juliet. How art thou out of breath when thou hast
    breath
To say to me that thou art out of breath?
Th' excuse that thou dost make in this delay
Is longer than the tale thou dost excuse.
Is thy news good or bad? Answer to that.
Say either, and I 'll stay the circumstance.
Let me be satisfy'd, is 't good or bad?
 Nurse. Well, you have made a simple choice, you
know not how to choose a man. Romeo? No, not he.
Though his face be better than any man's, yet his leg
excels all men's—and for a hand and a foot and a
body, though they be not to be talk'd on, yet they
are past compare. He is not the flower of courtesy,
but I 'll warrant him as gentle as a lamb. Go thy
ways, wench, serve God. What! have you din'd at
home?
 Juliet. No, no. But all this did I know before.

Juliet
—XL to meet
—Peter X-SL

← XL & sit
chair

—X to nurse
& kneel in
front of t
—up & DSR

WARNING

FRIAR
ROMEO

turn back &
X to her

A page of a prompt book prepared from a printed script.

script page is cut out of the middle of the looseleaf paper.
Then the script is taped in. The script is printed on both
sides. If you just taped it on a looseleaf page, you would
only see one side. A first-time stage manager solved this
problem by using two scripts. It worked all right, but it
cost twice as much money.

The stage directions are written in standard symbols
for blocking. The symbols for blocking correspond to certain positions on the stage. The stage is divided roughly
into six areas. Think of it as a tick-tack-toe game.

The diagram on the next page will help you.

All blocking is indicated from the actors' point of view.
When you are standing on a stage, facing the audience,

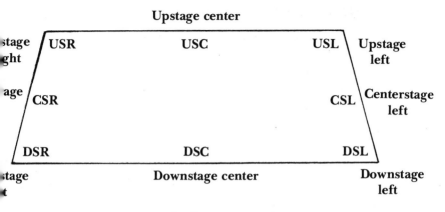

and the director tells you to, "Move downstage right," you will move down (to the front of the stage toward the audience) and to your right.

The director is the one who has to think in reverse when he or she faces the stage. When the director tells an actor to cross downstage left (XDSL), he or she must remember that the actor will move to the actor's left. This will be the director's right side.

Even the most experienced directors get confused sometimes. Don't let yourself get bogged down with stage directions or the prompt book. The book is meant as an aid to the actors and the director. No one can remember all the action, cues, etc. unless they are written down. Sometimes you have more blocking to remember than lines. The S.M. writes all blocking in pencil at first. The director may change his or her mind (directors do it all the time even on Broadway) so the S.M. keeps track of the latest blocking. After you have done a few plays, the stage directions become familiar to you. So don't worry about it. Think of the S.M.'s written direction as a road map to show you the way.

THE ASSISTANT DIRECTOR

Some directors like to use an assistant director, while others do not. It is up to each individual director. In amateur theater, it is a good idea to have an assistant director. He or she can assist with any number of jobs including playing one of the acting roles if necessary. Most people like the idea of being an assistant director better than being an understudy.

Some people think an assistant director is more important than the stage manager. Although it may sound more important, both jobs are equally necessary.

"It's what you make it!" commented a community theater director. "It's how I started out. I did every backstage job . . . and then some, but I learned about the theater. Now I can do any job there is."

One of the things an assistant director can do is take over some of the administrative tasks for the director. He or she can assist the stage manager at rehearsals and performances. With a large cast, it is essential to have both an assistant director and a stage manager, too.

Both the A.D. (assistant director) and the S.M. are responsible to the director. The actors are responsible to the director and sometimes to the assistant director. The director can assign the actors to work with the A.D.

Some directors assign the assistant director the responsibility of supervising the non-production elements of the play. These are called *front-of-house jobs* and include publicity, programs, box office, tickets, ushers, etc.

THE DIRECTOR

A highly successful woman director said, "Being a good director is just like being a good mother. If you do your job right, they won't need you anymore."

You may not agree with that, but one thing most people do agree on is that the director's job is the most difficult of all. The director is the boss. He or she must set down the ground rules from the beginning. There are as many different styles of directing as there are directors.

One professional director calls himself "a benevolent dictator." He tells his cast exactly what to do and when to do it. "I know what I want, and I tell them," he said sternly, "and if they don't give it to me, I—" He drew a finger across his throat but with a smile.

Another director said, "I let the actors flounder until they realize they need me, then I step in and save the day. That way I'm a hero."

Still another said, "I tell the actors exactly what I want from them in the very beginning and let them find it for themselves."

There are a variety of ways in which directors work. You will find the approach that works best for you. Directors are in agreement on one thing, however. Preparation is essential! Directors must do their homework before they even start rehearsals.

"I didn't know what homework was until I started directing plays for the drama club," said one high-school director. "I did more historic research on one play than I did all year in history class."

The first thing a director does is read the script. Then he asks himself some questions. Is it exciting? Does it fire the imagination? Can you hardly wait to get started? Do you see scenes that come to life in your imagination? Do you feel positive and enthusiastic about the script? Decide whether the play is worth the time and effort of everyone concerned. In other words, is the play worth doing? If the answer to all these questions is "Yes," do that play.

Needless to say, a group of people who get along well together have the best chance for a successful production. (It's unlike the professional theater where an actress can play a torrid love scene with her leading man onstage, but she doesn't speak to him offstage.)

Each person's job in the play must be carefully spelled out. There must be no misunderstanding of who is responsible for what. (Chapter 3 will go into more detail on this subject.)

Organization is the very heart of play production. Nowhere else is the success or failure of an event so totally dependent on each person individually . . . one at a time.

- If the spotlight comes on at exactly the right time, it's because the light person brought up the switch at that moment.
- If the window opens just right, it's because the set crew built it properly.
- If a breakaway coat tears perfectly where it is supposed to, it's because someone on the costume crew prepared it correctly.
- If the doorbell rings on cue to announce the arrival of a character, it's because the sound person made it happen at the right time.
- If the dialogue flows just as it would in life, it's because each player knows his or her lines perfectly.

A production should go smoothly when everyone does the job and works together as part of the whole. Just think what would happen to a play if each of the above jobs were not done correctly or at the right time. Sometimes things go wrong even when they have been carefully worked out. Then the actor learns to cope with the unexpected—another reason why the theater is such good practice for life.

Now that you've decided you want to do a particular play, decide if your group can do it. Be realistic about your capabilities or at least about how much you are willing to work. Ask yourself the following questions: Is it the play for your group? Can the group be successful with this particular script? Do you, or does the director, feel confident with the script? (Chapter 7 deals with directing in greater detail.)

What about time? Is there enough time to do the play? How much rehearsal time you have is as important as the script itself. Longer plays take more time to prepare than shorter ones. Musicals take more time than straight plays. You need enough time to schedule rehearsals so that your actors and crews will feel confident with the play or musical.

Hopefully, the play you select will excite everyone else as much as it excites you. That way, everyone is eager to work.

Now that you are organized for production, you are ready to spell out the responsibilities of each person involved.

It's time to plan ahead.

Chapter 3

A Role for Everyone

THE ACTORS

Do you want to act? Here's where you'll get a resounding "Yes" from the majority of the group. You'll find out that acting is the job most everyone wants.

"You always find more 'hams' than 'techies,' " groaned one set designer. (A "techie" is the one who works on the technical aspects of theater.)

What most people don't know about acting is how much hard work is involved. All they see are the actors onstage. What they don't see are the hours of rehearsal time and the additional hours spent learning lines and developing characterization.

Many beginners think all you have to do to act is learn lines. That may be the first step, but there's a lot more to it than that.

"I get mad every time I hear somebody say that acting is just showing off. It's a lot more than that. It's like giving a little piece of yourself every time you go out on stage," one young actress explained.

Every professional actor knows you start to work *after* you learn your lines. And every actor has had the nightmare of being onstage and going blank (forgetting the lines and not being able to think of anything to say).

"I remember coming onstage in act I and saying my opening line for act II which was, 'I come for pay.' The other actor looked confused but managed a gulp and said, 'You haven't worked for me yet. Go back and do some work first.' That gave me an excuse to go off, get my line, and come back. Then I started the scene over with the right line. I can laugh about it now," the actor said and chuckled, "but it was awful when it happened."

Actors worried about going blank as far back as Shakespeare's time:

> Like a dull actor now,
> I have forgot my part and I am out,
> Even to a full disgrace.
> *Coriolanus*
> ACT V, SCENE 3, LINE 40

Most directors prefer to work with actors before they memorize their lines. However, there are times when actors must know their lines before rehearsals begin. This happens when there is very little rehearsal time such as in summer stock. (The actors often do a new play every week.) But that is the exception.

Usually, the first meeting after the play is cast (see Chapter 8) is called the *first read through*. At this meeting, the actors sit down with the director and read through the play. Then they discuss it and ask questions. Why does he say this when he really means just the exact opposite? Why does he run away? What does she mean by that?

Some directors will answer the actors' questions for

them. And some will make the actors find the answers for themselves. "Dig for it!" Think it out yourself.

Let's say you're an actor. At the first read through you get an idea of how the play sounds. It sounds different when you hear other voices reading the play than when you read it by yourself. Then you only imagined others speaking the parts. This time you actually hear them.

Most directors like to finish blocking the play before they ask for "lines." It's easier to learn the words when you have a movement to associate with the lines. Your cue may be another actor reaching for a box; you have to walk quickly across to him and say, "No, don't touch that."

If you learn your lines in order, one after the other, that line might come after, "Oh, what a lovely day." The only way you could remember that would be by rote (like learning multiplication tables). It's much easier to learn lines with movement and association.

Professional actors get their "words" down as soon as possible. They spend whatever amount of time is necessary. They want to know the lines so well that they can say them in their sleep. Actors want those lines to sound so natural they don't have to think about them. Some actors spend many anguished hours committing lines to memory, but you'd never know it when you see them onstage. Be sure to learn all the lines, even the ones where you're supposed to read a letter or note. You can be sure at some performance that the lines on the paper will be missing, or some joker will write something on the paper like "your fly is open" or some other gag.

Actors use different ways to remember lines. Some learn each word exactly. Others get the general idea first and then work to be more exact. One good way to learn lines is to ask another person to "cue" you. (He reads the lines before yours, so that you hear the cue spoken before you say the line.) Keep going over the lines with someone cueing you until you know them.

Some actors tape-record their cues. They leave blank spaces on the tape where their lines are. Then they play the tape over and over until they know their lines and can keep the flow of dialogue moving at the correct pace.

Other actors sit with their scripts and cover their own lines with a card or their hand. They read their cues and then say their lines without looking. Then they lift the card to see if they said it correctly. If not, they go back and try again.

"I'm not a quick study," laments a well-known actress. "It takes me forever to learn my words."

There is no guaranteed way to learn lines that works for everyone. After you have learned lines a few times, you will find the method that works best for you. It might be a combination of methods.

Actors are responsible for knowing their lines and blocking. The director will usually set a deadline for lines to be memorized. Actors must attend every rehearsal, plus coming for any additional work that the director requests.

There's an old saying in the theater: "There's only one excuse for missing a rehearsal. That's a death in the family . . . preferably your own."

BACKSTAGE JOBS

The Set Designers

If you're going to do your play on a stage, you'll need more people involved in addition to the actors and director. Let's think about the stage. It doesn't have to be a raised platform with a curtain at one end. It can be any open space used as a playing area. It can be in your basement, a room at church, or even a classroom. But, if you have a traditional auditorium stage available, you'll probably want to use that. With that stage, you'll want a set or some suggestion for the environment of the play.

When you use any kind of set, no matter how simple, you will need someone to be responsible for it. He or she may build it or put together various set pieces to suggest a place. That person is the set designer or technical director. In amateur theater, it's usually the same person. The one who designs the set builds it with whatever help is available.

The T.D. (technical director) is in charge of "doing the set." That can be anything from putting a table and chairs on the stage to a totally reproduced living room with a moose head on the wall, rugs on the floor, lamps, etc. Your best bet is to keep it as simple as possible.

"You'd be amazed at what you can do with cardboard. Give me a mattress carton or a refrigerator box, and I can do a great set," one techie claimed. "It might not be Broadway, but it sure serves the purpose."

A professional set designer advised, "It's better to do a simple thing well than attempt a complicated one and do a lousy job."

The kind of play selected dictates how your set will be done. That's another consideration when you select the play. Don't pick a play that demands a complicated set and elaborate costumes unless you have a large budget and experienced people with the ability to create these things. Don't underestimate plain curtains for the set. Let your audience use their imaginations. They enjoy it. Even with a large budget, it's better to start out simply. You can move up to more complicated production elements after you've had some experience with play production.

Very often, "simpler means better" because it is more creative.

The set designer begins at the same point as the director and actors—with the script. He or she reads it to get the initial impact. The set will provide the environment for the actors. The entrances and exits will determine the blocking patterns, so the designer must confer with the director before beginning to design.

Some designers start with a real place and cut it down to its simplest form. Still others use the setting to illustrate an idea. They use a symbol or visual image to show the meaning of the play.

One of the pitfalls for beginners staging a play is too much emphasis on production elements. You can find yourself spending all your time on those areas and not enough on the play or the acting. Remember that nobody goes to see a play just for the set. You can go to a museum for a perfectly reproduced example of an ancient Egyptian palace. Don't try to create one on stage.

One famous set designer said, "You can suggest anything in this world . . . or any other . . . on the stage. It's when you try to make a set look exactly like something else—that's when you run into trouble."

The fact to keep in mind when planning your production is: Keep it simple.

Lights and Special Effects

There's nothing more exciting than when the house lights dim and go out momentarily. You know something special is going to happen. The suspense is thrilling to the audience and the actors. The lights come up and focus the audience's attention on another world onstage. Lights can have an almost hypnotic effect.

But don't get carried away. The most important function of stage lighting is to illuminate the stage. In other words, stage lights are meant to "shed light on the subject." If you can't see it, you can't believe it. You can create all kinds of moods and environments with light. But you must see the actors, or it won't matter what they do or how they do it.

Lights should illuminate the acting areas and focus attention on the important elements of the play. Light can shape the playing area to reinforce the stage picture.

If you're playing in the basement or a classroom, don't worry about stage lights. After all, theater began without artificial light centuries ago and played to capacity crowds in the daylight. At least you will have simple overhead lights.

Special effects such as fire, fog, and smoke are usually made with light. Fire can be suggested by red gelatin paper over a light. Fog can be made with dry ice and a fan

The director points out where a light should be hung to illuminate a particular area of the stage.

with a white light on it. Smoke can be done the same way with gray light on it. But be careful. Don't make it so realistic that someone calls the fire department!

If you want to learn more about stage lighting or get an idea of what special effects are available commercially, look at one or more of the books and catalogues listed in the "Sources of Materials" in the back of this book.

The rule to remember with stage lighting is: Let there be light!

The Costume Designer

Costumes must project the overall design of the mood of the play. The costume is very important to the actor psychologically. Put on a feather boa and see how it makes you feel, or put on a tight clerical collar. Get the idea? Costumes help create the character and the feeling of what the character is like.

An actress may swing her long skirt to accent her feeling of joy. An actor may grab at his necktie and rip it off to emphasize his irritation. The accent of a belt, collar, or ruffle can perk up an otherwise colorless dress. Look around in your basement or attic. Old curtains make wonderful overskirts. Aluminum foil is great for a robot costume. Once you start thinking about using what you find for costumes, you'll see dozens of possibilities. Remember that old saying: "One man's trash is another man's treasure."

There is a well-known theater group for young people called The Paper Bag Players. This company uses rolls of brown paper, paper bags, and cardboard boxes for all their sets and costumes. They start with a basic leotard and add whatever else they need with paper. What they come up with is often more believable than the standard sets and costumes of other groups who spend lots of money.

Again, remember your time restrictions. If you decide to make the costumes, give yourself plenty of time. Even people who sew well make mistakes when they are rushed. Although costumes must be sturdy, no one can see a seam from the audience. Dressmaker details are unnecessary on the stage.

Thrift shops are marvelous sources for costumes. Look for flea markets and garage sales in your area. It might not be the exact dress you're looking for, but with some fixing up, it would do. It might serve as the basic item from which to "build" the perfect costume. (Costume designers say they "build" costumes just as other designers build sets and bridges.)

A good rule to keep in mind for costumes is: Suggest the effect. Don't try for perfection.

Make-up

No costume is complete without the addition of make-up. Make-up is an extension of the costume. Sometimes it is more important for the actor psychologically than it is for the audience. Skillful coordination of make-up and costume is essential.

Make-up is vital when you perform under stage lights. Lights make the actors' faces look washed out and featureless. Every actor needs make-up, so that the audience can see his features and expressions. Make-up is meant to accent and emphasize.

When an actor plays a character different from himself in age or looks, he needs a different kind of make-up. That kind of make-up is called *character make-up*. One look

ACCESSORIES & PROPS

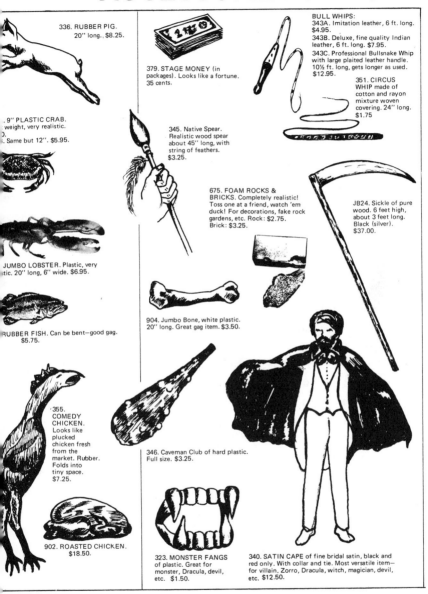

336. RUBBER PIG. 20" long, $8.25.

379. STAGE MONEY (in packages). Looks like a fortune. 35 cents.

BULL WHIPS:
343A. Imitation leather, 6 ft. long. $4.95.
343B. Deluxe, fine quality Indian leather, 6 ft. long. $7.95.
343C. Professional Bullsnake Whip with large plaited leather handle. 10½ ft. long, gets longer as used. $12.95.

351. CIRCUS WHIP made of cotton and rayon mixture woven covering. 24" long. $1.75

9" PLASTIC CRAB. weight, very realistic. . Same but 12". $5.95.

345. Native Spear. Realistic wood spear about 45" long, with string of feathers. $3.25.

675. FOAM ROCKS & BRICKS. Completely realistic! Toss one at a friend, watch 'em duck! For decorations, fake rock gardens, etc. Rock: $2.75. Brick: $3.25.

JB24. Sickle of pure wood. 6 feet high, about 3 feet long. Black (silver). $37.00.

JUMBO LOBSTER. Plastic, very tic. 20" long, 6" wide. $6.95.

904. Jumbo Bone, white plastic. 20" long. Great gag item. $3.50.

RUBBER FISH. Can be bent—good gag. $5.75.

355. COMEDY CHICKEN. Looks like plucked chicken fresh from the market. Rubber. Folds into tiny space. $7.25.

346. Caveman Club of hard plastic. Full size. $3.25.

902. ROASTED CHICKEN. $18.50.

323. MONSTER FANGS of plastic. Great for monster, Dracula, devil, etc. $1.50.

340. SATIN CAPE of fine bridal satin, black and red only. With collar and tie. Most versatile item— for villain, Zorro, Dracula, witch, magician, devil, etc. $12.50.

A page from Rubies Costume Company 1981 Catalog, used by permission of Rubies Costume Company, Inc.

in the mirror after you're made up as a witch will give you that extra belief in yourself as that character.

Character make-up includes such things as lines, shadows, haircolors, putty noses, false hair, etc. This kind of make-up can create a totally different person from the actor playing the role.

Remember that the object of make-up is to look natural on the stage. For the best results with make-up, keep in mind that too little is better than too much. There's nothing worse than being aware of the make-up on an actor. If make-up calls attention to itself, it defeats the purpose unless, of course, it is used for some attention-getting device.

"Shave it off or pencil it in," a director said to one young man who immediately penciled in the mustache he was trying to grow.

It must have worked because one young lady in the audience said, "I can't believe that's George. He looks so old."

Wigs and masks add believability to certain characters. Most make-up houses stock a full line of these extras.

Make-up can do many different things in addition to creating a natural appearance. Masks can be painted on faces, as well as wearing the traditional face mask. Wigs can change the entire appearance of an actor or actress.

Special make-up sessions before dress rehearsals will make things much easier for everyone involved. Any intricate make-up designs, such as false noses, scars, painted face masks, etc., should be practiced well ahead of time. Order enough supplies of your special materials to see you through the last night of performance.

Some groups use masks as part of their production approach, while others create wigs and make-up for themselves. The Paper Bag Players make use of wigs and masks made from paper bags.

The rule for make-up is: Less is better.

Sound

Most plays call for the use of some sound effects. It can be as simple as a door buzzer or as complicated as the sound of a roaring ocean with sea gulls in the background.

An interesting thing about sound is that you believe what you think you hear. If an actor drops a glass, and it falls behind a sofa with a sound of breaking glass, you believe the glass is broken. You thought you saw it and you *heard* it. But it was a sound effect. You can't be sure the glass will break every night, so you use a sound effect. Many sounds are not what they seem, but they give the desired effect.

In the old days before electronic recordings, sounds were made in a variety of inventive ways. Rain was suggested by dropping dried peas on a drum. Thunder was made by rattling a thin metal sheet.

It is also important for the sound effect to be heard at the right time. Nothing shatters the illusion of reality onstage as much as a missed or late sound cue. You've probably seen one of the classic examples of this when an actor said, "I thought I heard the telephone ring . . ." Then the telephone rings. That tells everyone—loud and clear—that somebody goofed!

An actor in a murder mystery had to shoot someone onstage. The blank in the gun didn't fire. Instead of improvising some other method of murder, the actor said "Bang." You can imagine what happened to that tragic moment. It brought down the house with laughter. The whole illusion was shattered.

There are two common ways of doing sound effects. One method is to have everything on tape. Your sound person is responsible for all the cues. He relies on his technical know-how to collect or create and record the sounds. Once he has all his sounds on tape, he's ready to mark and cue them. He must know exactly what comes when. There are commercially prepared sound effect records and tapes which you can buy. You will find those sources in the back of this book. You can find practically anything on commercial sound effect records, from a roaring train going into a tunnel to a full-scale air battle with machine gun fire or rare bird calls in a tropical forest. These sounds would be difficult for most amateurs to locate and tape for themselves.

"The most difficult sound effect I ever had to come up with was a gurgling sink," a young techie said. "It couldn't be just any kind of gurgle, it had to be something special and was vital to the play *Dumbell People in a Barbell World.*" He laughed remembering his frustration. "I tried everything from a flushing toilet to a growling stomach. Nothing worked. Finally, I got the sound by putting several things together: sloshing water, banging a pipe . . . I forget what else, but it sounded great—just like a gurgling sink should."

Some sound cues are done "live." Someone pushes the button installed outside the entrance door for the door bell. A loud crash is made by someone dropping several tin cans in a metal waste bin.

Whenever possible, each actor is responsible for his own sound cues.

No matter what sound effect method you choose, make sure it's carefully cued to the right time. Double check every mechanical device on stage. Make sure it is in good working order. Check and re-check. Is the gun loaded with blanks? Sound cues must be rehearsed until they are perfect. Don't put an actor in the position of saying "Gee, I think I hear a thundering herd of elephants coming this way."

The rule for sound effects is: Repeat until perfect every time.

Props

Props can range from an ashtray to an oversized bass fiddle case. You sometimes run into the controversy of whether some object is a prop or set piece. Frequently it can be either. One easy way to define a prop is: "any object that can be held in the hand." It is generally carried on stage by an actor. It can also be placed on stage by the prop person for the actor to pick up sometime during the scene. It can be carried off by the actor or removed when the curtain is down or during a blackout. Set pieces are usually larger than props and remain permanently on the set.

"But I can carry on a chair," an actor will say, "or even a small table. Does that make it a prop?" It is not a prop because it is part of the set.

Don't be too concerned with the distinction. The only time it becomes a problem is when the set crew says, "It's a prop. Let the prop crew do it."

And the prop crew head says, "It's set. Let the set crew do it."

Then it's time for the director to step in and say, "I consider it a prop (or whatever). *You* do it!" That settles the question. The director always has the final word. He or she makes the decision.

Most props can be borrowed or made. If the first two choices fail, then buy them. Remember that it doesn't have to be the real thing. A cardboard box painted gold looks like a real gold box on stage.

Sometimes all it takes is a little ingenuity and imagination to make a particular prop. A cardboard star painted silver on the end of a stick with bits of glass glued to it makes a perfect magic wand.

As magicians say, "It's not a trick, it's *illusion.*"

Some plays call for strange or unusual props that can test your ingenuity to the fullest.

"I once had to turn straw into gold onstage before your very eyes," a director said, "and if you think that's easy, you're crazy!"

"Well, how did you do it?" someone asked.

"A flip-top basket. The straw was secured to one side, and it was flipped over with the gold on the other. We got a gasp from the audience every time."

One designer once made a fancy French telephone from some pieces of pipe. Onstage, it looked exactly like the real thing.

When people know you're putting on a play, especially if it's a local group, they're usually willing to help out. If you need a straight jacket for *The House of Blue Leaves,* go to a psychiatric hospital and ask to borrow one. You can approach local merchants, friends, and members of the community to borrow props or set pieces. Give them a credit in the program. Everyone likes to see his name in print. And it's also good publicity.

A word of caution—when you borrow something, treat it with extra-special care. Be careful not to break or damage the item in any way. If you do break something, replace it. Don't wait to be asked. Don't ruin your chances or the chance for others who might follow in your foot-

The seats should be placed so that everyone in the audience can see the stage.

steps to borrow something another time. Goodwill can't be bought, it must be earned.

Again, if your production depends on a certain prop, which cannot be borrowed or made, there are prop companies that rent props and/or create anything you can imagine. This is usually more expensive than most amateurs can handle. You will find some prop houses listed in the back of the book.

The rule to remember is: The illusion is what counts.

Front of House

Front of house refers to those jobs which are not done onstage or backstage. These are important non-acting jobs. These people come in contact with the audience first. That means they set the tone of the performance. If the audience has a pleasant experience at the box office, with the ticket taker and the ushers, they are in the mood to enjoy the performance.

You need a pleasant, smiling person in the box office, one who is efficient and has a lot of patience. You need ushers who will listen to the playgoer's preference in seating and try to accommodate them whenever possible.

One director gives this advice to the front-of-house staff: "Treat every member of the audience like he or she is a guest in your home."

Publicity-Promotion

At least two weeks before the play opens, you should publicize the event. The planning must be done earlier. Put one person in charge. He or she can delegate jobs to other people if additional help is required.

Most local or school newspapers will be glad to run an interesting picture of your cast in rehearsal. The more interesting or unique the picture, the better chance there is to see it in print.

A simple, straightforward article can accompany the picture. Your article or *press release* should include:

1. Names of the cast, director, and others involved
2. The name of the play and the author
3. Where the play will be held
4. Production dates and times
5. Ticket information

You may want to include something about the play. Give information that will make people want to see it. For example, "This is the play that made John Travolta a star," or "This is the play that has been running for 20 years in London."

You will need posters to put up in school, in local store windows, and anywhere else where your potential audience will see them. You may want to make flyers to hand out to your family and friends. Both posters and flyers include the same basic information as the news release. You may want to add a drawing, logo, or some other kind of attention-getting device.

Again, there are packaged publicity kits available on certain shows. You merely fill in the information on your production. The information regarding the play itself is already printed on the posters.

Program

The program is prepared in plenty of time to be ready for opening night. Give yourself some insurance and have it ready for your preview. The program includes all the information on your press release and flyer. It also lists all the characters in the play and the actors who are playing them. It tells where the play takes place and when. It lists the names of the crews and everyone who worked on the play. Double check names for the correct spellings.

Make sure to give credit and/or special thanks to those who donated props or costumes. Give special thanks to anyone outside the group who was particularly helpful with the production.

Your program can be a simple sheet printed on one side or the standard folded program, which has four sides. You might want to come up with your own original pro-

Tickets can be as imaginative and creative as any other part of the production.

gram with art work. As long as you include the essential information, you can be as artistic and creative as you like.

Tickets

Tickets add a positive psychological effect to your entire production. Not only do they grant the right of admission, but they also add an element of anticipation. You don't have to use a standard printed ticket. This is another area where you can add your own creativity.

Sell your tickets beforehand if possible. That helps with publicity, too. It gets people to notice the project and, hopefully, to start talking about it.

You're probably thinking that you never realized there were so many non-acting jobs in doing a play. There are many people involved in play production. A lot of these people you never see, but they are equally as important as the ones onstage.

Once you understand what has to be done, organize your group to do it. Make sure everyone knows what job or jobs he or she has to do. The more carefully you organize the work, the more fun you can have, and the more successful the whole production will be.

Chapter 4

What Type of Play?

"I love every play I've ever seen," admitted one young actress. "Of course, that's not very many, but still—how can I choose one?"

Pick a play you like, a play that excites you.

Pick a play that you and your group are enthusiastic about, one you really want to do.

And pick a play that you and your group *can* do.

Easy enough, right? The first two instructions are simple. But how can you tell if the play you select is one you *can* do?

To find out, ask the following questions:

1. Is it a good script? Does it tell an interesting and exciting story?
2. Can you cast your play?
3. Does the play have interesting roles?

4. Will the play maintain the interest of everyone concerned?
5. Do you have enough time to do the play? How much rehearsal will it take?
6. Can your group afford to do the play? How much will it cost?
7. Can you meet the physical demands of the play (set, costumes, technical effects)?
8. Is there an audience for this play?
9. Do you feel a sense of adventure and challenge with the play?
10. Is the play worth doing?

If your answer to these ten questions is "Yes," you've picked the right one.

A spokesman for the play publisher Samuel French, Inc., lists their dozen most popular full-length plays for the amateur market:

1. *Our Town*
2. *Barefoot in the Park*
3. *Story Theatre*
4. *The Mousetrap*
5. *Charley's Aunt*
6. *Thurber's Carnival*
7. *Spoon River Anthology*
8. *Blithe Spirit*
9. *Plaza Suite*
10. *The Matchmaker*
11. *The Miracle Worker*
12. *Ah, Wilderness!*

Before you select your play, consider several things. You must write to the publisher to obtain permission to put on the play. Permission is not automatically granted and you should obtain it before proceeding farther.

BUDGET

Let's stop for a moment and think about the cost of a play. When do you have to spend money? And when do you have choices?

First, if you are doing a published play, you must buy scripts for everyone. If it is a play that is not available in a published script, you will have to make copies for your actors. Either way, it is an item that must be figured into your budget.

Some plays are royalty free but most are not. A royalty is the money you pay to the publisher for permission to put on the play. (The publisher pays part of this to the playwright.) You pay a set amount for each performance of the play. For example, the royalty on the play *The Mousetrap* is $50–25. That means that you must pay a royalty of $50 for the first performance and $25 for each additional performance. If you plan to do the play three times, the royalty is $100 (one @ $50 and two @ $25). The royalty for each play is listed in the play catalog.

You must budget for costumes, props, set, make-up, lights, sound, etc. These are called production costs. Other items must be considered also. You will need to budget for publicity, tickets, and programs.

Hopefully, you may be able to make and/or borrow many of the items on your production budget. The following sample budget assumes that you will, because it is low. It is for a full-length play put on at school. It is assumed that lighting and sound equipment are already there.

Production Costs

scripts (10 @ $2.50)	$ 25.00
royalty	100.00
set	150.00
props	50.00
sound	10.00
light (gels only)	10.00
make-up	25.00
costumes	50.00
Sub-total	$420.00

Additional Costs

publicity		$100.00
(pictures, flyers, press releases, etc.)		
programs		50.00
tickets		25.00
miscellaneous		50.00
(There's always some expense that you didn't anticipate)		
	Sub-total	$225.00
		420.00
		225.00
	Total	$645.00

It's a good idea to plan a budget first, even if you have only $50 to spend. You don't have to stick to the budget exactly, but it is a guide to help you remember the areas in which you will need money.

Of course, a shorter play put on in someone's basement will not have the same costs. But you can be sure that it will cost something. On the other hand, if you're doing a public performance of a musical with many scenes, your budget will be much higher.

ONE-ACT PLAYS

What kind of play is the easiest one for beginners to perform? There is no right answer to this question. A lot depends on individual likes and dislikes. But a good one-act play with a variety of interesting characters can be exactly what you're looking for. It can be an excellent choice for a first play production.

A one-act play offers a shorter script than the standard

full-length play, which has two or three acts. This means the one-act play runs about an hour. Two- or three-act plays run around two hours. (Give or take twenty minutes, either way.) Since the playing time is shorter, you will need less rehearsal time for a one-act play. There aren't as many lines and the actors' parts will be smaller.

The royalty on one-act plays is less than on a full-length play. The one-act is usually done in one set. Frequently, longer plays call for several scene changes.

Many amateur groups put on a bill of two one-act plays for a full evening of entertainment. Some are even published that way, like *The White Liars* and *Black Comedy*. This gives more people the opportunity to participate and to play larger roles. You can find one-act plays with casts from two to fifteen.

Play catalogs are the best source for all play selection. Plays are listed by types such as one-acts, full-lengths, musicals, children's plays, holiday plays, religious plays, etc. Each title is followed by a paragraph which gives information about the play. It gives you a short synopsis of the play plus the type: comedy, drama, farce, etc.

Some catalogs will tell you what kinds of groups the play is best suited for. Some of the suggested groups are little theater (community theater), high school, college, all groups. This tells you something about the level of difficulty in putting on a play. The listing will also tell you how many sets are needed, whether they are interior (int.) or exterior (ext.). It will give you further information as to how many characters and their sex. You will see it written like this: 1M, 2F, and 1C. That means the cast of the play has one male, two females and one child.

The page reproduced from a Samuel French, Inc. catalog shows how the symbols work.

FULL-LENGTH PLAYS

What if you decide to do a full-length play? Is it really that much harder? Does it take a lot more work?

The full-length play takes more time to rehearse than the one-act. It may take more than one set. Usually, the royalty will be higher. This kind of play will take more of everything, most especially, time and money.

You do have a greater selection, however. And most well-known plays fall into this category. A well-known title helps at the box office.

The full-length play offers greater challenges for your actors. They must sustain their characterizations over a longer period of time. And they have more lines to learn.

One director said, "Both types of plays take the same amount of effort. For that reason, I choose to begin with the full-length play."

The most difficult show to do is the musical. It demands all the production elements of the full-length play plus several more. Most musicals call for more scenery and more elaborate costumes. Of course, there are exceptions like *The Fantasticks* which has only eight characters.

The royalty on a musical is higher than on either the one-act or the full-length play. With a musical, not only do you pay royalties on the book but also on the music and lyrics.

A musical demands more directorial help. You need a musical director, a choreographer, a rehearsal pianist, and sometimes an orchestra and conductor.

You must plan on spending a lot more time on a musical than on a straight play. Songs and dances must be rehearsed along with the book (the play part). When all to sell Phil to the matriarch and unsell Spencer Grant, Back Bay scion engaged to Claire. They're too successfull— Mary realizes she still loves Phil and so they have to reverse themselves. Claire—realizing she'd never be happy with Phil's kind of carefree life marries Spencer after all. And Phil realizes he and Mary belong together. "Funny and witty . . . greatly gleeful."—N.Y. American. In mss. (Royalty, $25-$20.)   (**#10080**)

THE SNOB. (Little Theatre.) Comedy. Carl Sternheim. Translated by Eric Bentley. 4 m., 4 f. 3 int. The drama of a commanding young man who knows exactly what he wants and how he'll get it. He's about to be appointed president of the large corporation he now serves as secretary. Clearing the tracks—he pays off handsomely his mistress without a touch of human feeling and yet not unkindly. In a similar manner, he does the same with his parents, sending them abroad lest they embarrass him. A fascinating portrait of a shrewd, ruthless man dedicated to ambition. In *From The Modern Repetoire, Series I.* $12.50. (Royalty $25-$20.)   (**#21240**)

THE CHINESE PRIME MINISTER. (Little Theatre.) Comedy. Enid Bagnold. 5 m., 3 f. Int. Miss Bagnold's first play since *The Chalk Garden* "shimmers on the stage like a vast insubstantial spider's web, strung with bits of real rain." (N.Y. Herald Tribune). Margaret Leighton played the Broadway role of the aging actress who muses on the wisdom of age and the reverence for it in the days of ancient China. At one of her parties we finally meet her husband, an oil tycoon, and learn the secret of his departure many years before; and her two sons, one of whom is married to a rowdy wife, the other to a wayward one. All three marriages are given another breath of life through the play's action. But it is mostly what is written between the lines that raises this play to literary eminence. "I find myself touched, I think, because I have seen one whole play in which there is not a single careless line" . . . "A lovely play . . . A comedy that is adult, spirited, tender and humorously wise; a kind of autumnal shower of champagne."—N.Y. World-Telegram & Sun. $2.50. (Royalty, $50-$25.)   (**#5092**)

THE MOUSETRAP. (All Groups.) Melodrama. Agatha Christie. 5 m., 3 f. Int. The author of "Ten Little Indians" and "Witness for the Prosecution" comes forth with another English hit about a group of strangers stranded in a boarding house during a snow storm, one of whom is a murderer. The suspects include the newly married couple who run the house, and the suspicions that are planted in their minds nearly wreck their perfect marriage. Others are a spinster with a curious background, an architect who seems better equipped to be a chef, a retired Army rmajor, a strange little man who claims his car has overturned in a drift, and a feminine jurist who makes life miserable for everyone. Into their midst comes a policeman, traveling on skis. He no sooner arrives, than the jurist is killed. Two down, and one to go. To get to the rationale of the murderer's pattern, the policeman probes the background of everyone present, and rattles a lot of skeletons. Another famous Agatha Christie switch finish! Chalk up another superb intrigue for the foremost mystery writer of her half century. $2.50. Special Sound Record, $11.00. Special Sound Tape, $16. (Royalty, $50-$25.) **Posters and Publicity Kits.**   (**#10**)

NOT IN THE BOOK. (All Groups.) Comedy. Arthur Watkyn. 7 m., 1 f. Int. An enormously funny show exceptionally well suited for non-professional groups. This high-styled comedy from London introduces us to the respectable home of Andrew Bennett, and to his family and friends. Into the picture comes a South American intent on blackmailing Andrew with some knowledge of his rash youth on that continent. A certain unpublished novel gives Andrew the idea of poisoning the blackmailer, but at the last minute he suffers a severe attack of conscience, and warns the blackmailer not to drink the poison. But the blackmailer falls dead anyway, and the finger of guilt is pointed at Andrew. This, happily, is only the beginning of the investigation, for the inspector finds other victims of the blackmailer as well. Andrew will be a little more tolerant hereafter of others' mistakes. A sterling hit from England, thoroughly disarming in its humor. Wilfred Hyde White played the role of Andrew in the production at the Criterion Theatre. $2.50. (Royalty, $35-$25.)   (**#16040**)

LO AND BEHOLD! (All Groups.) Comedy. John Patrick. 5 m., 3 f. Int. This comedy has to do with a Nobel Prize Winner who has lived for many years on a meagre, unpalatable diet, to favor an ailing heart. This very lack of much heart has made the philosophy of his books coldly cynical. After signing a will that leaves a third of his estate to his young doctor, a third to perpetuate his house as a sanctuary for his spirit and the final third to the Harvard Law School to insure that the terms of his odd testament will be carried out, he eats a sumptuous meal and dies happily. Instead of the solitude he has expected to find, he is beset by the spirits of an Indian girl pushed off a cliff by her lover, a Southern belle with a disturbing drawl and a phony liberal attitude, and a frustrated composer. As if this weren't enough to annoy the soul of an aesthete, the pretty cook (a former model) who had prepared the fatal dishes, returns to the house and is mistaken for his illegitimate daughter. The author eventually finds peace in furthering a romance between the doctor and the young girl. Another sure-fire hit for those High Schools and Little Theatres that enjoyed "The Hasty Heart" and "The Curious Savage," by the same author. "Its idea is amusing and so are the players, and Patrick has learned the trick of inserting a big solid laugh line at the right moment."—Daily News. $2.50. (Royalty, $50-$25.)   (**#653**)

SPEAKING OF MURDER. (All Groups.) Melodrama. Audrey and William Roos. 3 m., 5 f. Int. When Charles Ashton brings home his second wife, he fails to notice the hate and jealousy in his secretary's eyes. Nor is he aware of the dangers that threaten his wife, as his secretary turns the full force of her malice upon her. Soon we know the shocking truth; it was she who killed the first wife. Now it is her intention to lock the second wife in a library vault, where it is calculated she will suffocate within two hours. A delightful old biddy who holds the solution in her hand and who might save the wife does not, unhappily, remain alive either. The key is left to the young stepson, and to justice. Will the vault be opened in time? "A pleasant shedunit."—N.Y. Daily Mirror. "A delightfully sinister evening in the theatre."— N.Y. Journal-American. "One of the vilest villainesses in recent literature . . . (can be) splendid fun."—N.Y. Herald Tribune. $2.50. (Royalty, $50-$25.)   (**#21280**)

A page from *Samuel French's Basic Catalogue of Plays*, used by permission of Samuel French, Inc.

of these individual areas are ready, they are put together and rehearsed as a whole.

"A word of warning here," an experienced stage director pointed out. "If you use a musical director, make sure you both agree on the whole concept of the musical. If the stage director has one idea of the interpretation of a song and the musical director has another, look out! That can cause havoc for all concerned."

One director of a children's acting company said, "I feel insecure with a musical. I have to rely on too many other people. You can't rehearse without them, which puts me in a panic . . . but I don't show it."

Another director takes the opposite view, "Musicals give an extra feeling. There's more movement. It's an extra way to get the point across. If you don't understand the play one way, you can understand it another way through the music and dance."

One thing both directors agree upon is the amount of effort necessary to put on a musical and the amount of self-discipline it takes on the part of all the performers.

"It's not magic. You must make the effort each time," said the children's director.

Is it worth it? "It's like putting together a jig-saw puzzle. But there's nothing else quite like it . . . when you pull it off. Doing a musical is great!" answered another director.

THEATER FOR YOUNG AUDIENCES

There's another kind of play you might consider. That's children's theater or theater for young people. This kind of production is aimed at a specific audience.

Frequently, this type of show combines elements of all

three of the other types of plays. You may have to look a little harder for a good script, but they are available. Some scripts like *A Christmas Carol* become traditions, and groups do them every year.

The length of a children's theater script is usually about the same as a one-act play (around an hour, but some play fifteen to thirty minutes longer).

Plays for children's theater offer a variety of colorful characters and locations. The characters are often from a world of fantasy. (Maximilian Productions, a New York City based children's theater group, did a play called *The Blue Planet* in which everybody and everything in that environment was blue.)

Fantasy can be very important in a world where so much emphasis is put on the scientific. Albert Einstein said, "The gift of fantasy has meant more to me than my talent for absorbing positive knowledge."

Royalties on a published children's theater script are somewhat less than on a full-length script.

Sets and costumes take more imagination and creativity, but they can usually be done with less money than those for the adult play.

The greatest advantage to doing this type of play is the audience. No other audience is as appreciative as children. Every actor will be a star in those youngsters' eyes. Children often line up for the actors' autographs after the show.

"There's no audience in the world like children. They let you know exactly what they think," an actor said, remembering his many happy experiences in children's theater.

Don't make the mistake of thinking that kind of show is easy. It's not. All the same standards of excellence found in adult theater are necessary in children's theater. In fact, your group has a greater responsibility when they play for children.

"If they like what they see, they will want to come back to the theater again and again. If not, well . . . who knows, you may have lost a potential theater-goer for life."

Only the best is good enough for children.

SPECIAL AUDIENCES

School Plays

What if you have to put on a play for a specific group? Does that affect your script selection? It certainly does! Don't choose a play like *The Four Poster*. It has two characters that grow old during the course of the play. Select a play that would appeal to your age group, like *Picnic* or *Grease*.

Pick a play that will offer a challenge to the actors, but one that your audience can identify with and will want to come to see. There's nothing worse than playing to an empty house. There's an old saying in the theater: "If there are more people on the stage than in the audience, cancel the performance."

Church Plays

You may want to put on a play in church for a specific purpose, for a holiday, or to teach a lesson. Since the middle ages the church has put on plays to teach moral lessons and Bible stories. The most famous church play, or morality play as it is called, is *Everyman.* This play is still being performed as it was in the 1500s.

The Samuel French Basic Catalog of Plays lists over fifty

Select a play that will appeal to your particular audience.

religious plays. And there are more play publishers who have others on their lists.

If you don't find what you want, it can be a most rewarding experience for a group to create their own script. (See Chapter 10.)

Camp Plays

Most camp plays are adapted from stories or created by and for the campers. These plays are aimed at a specific audience. It is literally "a captive audience." For that reason, creating your own play through improvisation (making up your own dialogue and actions spontaneously) and then scripting it is usually the best way to do a camp play. It certainly is less hectic.

Formal play production should be attempted only if you have the proper help and facilities and/or space. And, even then, most camp drama directors agree that it is advisable to create your own play. Of course, there are exceptions like the special performing arts, or drama camps, that specialize in putting on plays during the summer. These camps have professional directors and designers. But most camps offer a broad program without a specially trained drama person. This is where it's better to create your own play.

Everyone is closely associated at camp, since they live together for a certain period of time. That means there can be a lot of "in" jokes and situations. Most campers enjoy playing the roles of counselors and vice versa. Make use of that spirit of fun and parody. You can always "change the names to protect the innocent."

If you decide you would rather do a scripted play,

choose something simple. Try one the whole group likes and is enthusiastic about. Keep it fun and don't try to incorporate lavish production elements. You can use a few props and suggest costumes. Remember . . . "The play's the thing."

Classroom Plays

Let's say you have already decided against any of the one-act or full-length plays. For the classroom, you want something simple. You know there will be very little time to work on the play or to learn lines.

In that case, you might consider a play that is meant to be read aloud rather than performed. This type of play is called *readers' theater* or *script-in-hand performance.* These plays are in demand by groups who like to get up and read plays. But they don't have to learn lines or build sets and costumes. This technique is becoming increasingly popular with senior citizen groups. They enjoy doing plays, but many feel they can no longer remember lines.

There are collections of plays for readers' theater. Most of these plays are available to groups royalty free (when they are done in a classroom or group setting, and no admission is charged).

Of course, it's not all that hard to create your own readers' theater script from any standard one. Simply have one of your players function as a narrator. All stage directions are italicized in the script. The narrator can read the directions that are necessary for understanding the action as well as the descriptions of places and actions. The actors can read the lines of dialogue. It's best to rehearse it a few times if you plan on sharing it with an audience.

Plays for Living Room/Recreation

"Let's put on a show!"

Years ago, a lot of movies started out that way. There were several young, attractive people who were headed for Broadway, or so they thought. One of them always had a barn, and they turned that barn into a theater. By the end of the movie, they put on a lavish production. Everything was perfect.

Very few of us have a barn today . . . let alone an empty one. You're lucky if you have a basement, an attic, or a living room where you can put on a play.

All plays can be fun. However, when you do one for that reason, you have lots of options. You can think of it as a camp show or classroom play. You can use a short script or write your own. (See Chapter 10.) You can offer your family and friends some informal entertainment. This kind of drama activity has the greatest value for the performers, but an audience can enjoy your efforts.

Public Performance (Fund Raising)

Remember, when you charge admission you have a responsibility to the audience. Read over the discussion on script selection. When you put on a play for the public, you want to offer the very best production possible. Even if admission is free, you still have a responsibility to your audience. Time is valuable. If the audience is willing to spend their time watching your play, you must give them a valuable experience.

There are some types of plays that usually work for teenage actors. Just like the title of an old radio show said: "I love a mystery."

Mystery plays are good plays to perform. Most have a number of interesting, colorful characters. Mysteries offer an obvious problem, complications, and finally a solution or conclusion. There is suspense and action. Some offer scenes of physical daring and possible violence. (A stage fight takes hours of practice to do exactly right. But it's great fun.)

If you are in doubt about your choice of play, try a mystery. Everyone loves to figure out who did it.

Old-fashioned melodramas are fun to do. The main characters are always the same. There's a villain, a hero, and a heroine. Sometimes the heroine has a father or a guardian. Often there is a weak character who causes some of the trouble. Other characters add a dash of intrigue. For awhile, it looks as if all is lost for the heroine. Somehow the hero has been put out of the way momentarily. Just as the villain is about to triumph, the hero comes in—in the nick of time—and saves the day.

You may have seen the old monologue done by one person with a folded piece of paper to represent a bow. He puts the bow on his head for the heroine, under his nose as a mustache for the villain, and under his chin like a bow tie for the hero:

> VILLAIN: You must pay the rent.
> HEROINE: I can't pay the rent.
> VILLAIN: You must pay the rent.
> HEROINE: I can't pay the rent.
> HERO: I'll pay the rent.
> HEROINE: My hero!
> VILLAIN: Curses! Foiled again!

Encourage your audience to participate. Hiss the villain and cheer the hero. Melodramas are written in a very broad style and played as farce. Everyone knows good will triumph over evil. This style of play is a good choice for amateur groups.

Old Favorites

Some plays are well-known favorites. These are called "actor proof." (They're so good that they almost play by themselves.) Audiences want to see a play they remember, especially when they remember how much they liked it.

All you have to do is announce the title, and you've got an audience. Go back and look at the list given in the beginning of this chapter. Some other titles that always draw are: *Arsenic and Old Lace, The Odd Couple, Life with Father, The Skin of Our Teeth,* and *The Children's Hour.* Each of these plays has been done many times. They stand the test of time and are as good today as they were years ago when they were first produced. Any of these full-length plays could guarantee an audience because the title is so familiar.

There are certain musicals that seem to be done again and again. And people still flock to see them. A few of these titles are: *The King and I, Peter Pan, West Side Story, Oklahoma, South Pacific, Annie Get Your Gun, Godspell, The Me Nobody Knows, Fiddler on the Roof, You're a Good Man, Charlie Brown.*

To those lists of old favorites, add the following mysteries by Agatha Christie. Each of these is a good choice for an amateur group: *The Mousetrap, Ten Little Indians, The Unexpected Guest,* and *Murder on the Nile.*

You might want to add some melodramas that work well with teenage actors: *The Curse of an Aching Heart, The Drunkard, Dirty Work at the Crossroads, Egad, What a Cad!*

Some good one-act plays include: *Red Carnations, Heat Lightning, Something New in Murder, Two Crooks and a Lady.*

Now you know some of the pros and cons of different kinds of plays. Decide which type of play you want to do. Who will be your audience? After that, you're ready to make your play selection. The play must inspire as many hours of hard work as it takes to put on a good show. Remember the first rule: It must be a play you like—a play that excites you.

Read as many plays as it takes to find the one that is right for your group.

CHAPTER 5

Finding the Right Play

How do you find play scripts? You may be thinking, "I don't know what play I like until I read it."

You will find plays in the library. They are listed by title and author. In collections and anthologies, they can be found under subject (plays). There are collections of one-act plays, prize-winning plays, plays for all occasions, etc.

There are play indexes to consult in the library. These indexes will give you the information necessary to locate the play either in collections, anthologies, or in periodicals. These indexes are found in the reference section of your library. Some titles you might look for are:

- Chicorel, Marietta, ed. *Chicorel Theatre Index to Plays in Anthologies, Periodicals, Disks and Tapes.* New York: Chicorel, 1970.
- Keller, Dean H. *Index to Plays in Peridoicals.* Metuchen, N.J.: Scarecrow Press, 1971.
- Ottemiller, John. *Ottemiller's Index to Plays in Collections.* 6th ed., rev. and enl. Metuchen, N.J.: Scarecrow Press, 1976.

- *Play Index.* 1949–52, 1953–60, 1961–67, 1968–72, 1973– . New York: H. W. Wilson.
- Salem, James J. *Drury's Guide to Best Plays.* 2nd ed. Metuchen, N.J.: Scarecrow Press, 1969.

The only way to find the right play for your group is to read several of them. Some directors read twenty or thirty plays each time they make a selection.

You can usually tell at a glance if the play is suitable or not for your group. Check the character breakdown. (How

Musicals usually have large casts and can be expanded to involve more people by enlarging the chorus.

many males and how many females?) Check the subject matter. (Is it something that interests you and your group?) What are the set requirements?

If you know you have ten people who want to act, don't waste your time reading a play like *The Four Poster.* Remember it only has two characters.

When you consider a musical like *The Desert Song,* look carefully. You will note that this musical (operetta) has five exteriors and five interiors. That means it has five scenes which will be played outside and five scenes played inside. Some of the scenes can be doubled (with a little ingenuity), but you will need to build several sets. And, unless you have a very creative set designer, the cost may be too high. Consider how much it will cost and how much time it will take to create. This play is about the French military and the Arabs. That tells you immediately that certain costumes are essential. And there are seventeen principal characters.

You know that this show will take a good-sized budget, a long rehearsal period, and a lot of support personnel in addition to the set designer and costume designer. It needs a musical director, a choreographer, and a rehearsal pianist. If you are considering *The Desert Song* for a school play and have the money and people available, do it. It's a great show. But if you're working with a limited budget and a few people, forget this one. You can see at a glance, it's not for you. You don't have to read the whole play to make that decision.

One of the best ways to check a lot of plays at one time is with a catalog. Most high schools and/or public libraries have catalogs of plays. If you cannot find catalogs in your area, write to the publisher and request a catalog for your group or school.

The two biggest publishers of plays are:

Samuel French, Inc.
25 West 45th Street
New York, N.Y. 10036

Dramatists Play Service
440 Park Ave. South
New York, N.Y. 10016

Samuel French, Inc. also publishes musicals as does:

Tams-Witmark
Music Library, Inc.
757 Third Avenue
New York, N.Y. 10017

There are play publishers that specialize in certain types of plays. Some publishers gear their material for the high-school market. They list plays for all school productions, contest use, holidays, and special occasions:

Baker's Plays
100 Chauncy St.
Boston, Mass. 02111

The Dramatic Publishing Co.
4150 N. Milwaukee Ave.
Chicago, Ill. 60641

Some publishers are particularly well known for their plays for young people (children's theater and theater for youth):

New Plays, Inc.
Box 273
Rowayton, Ct. 06853

Anchorage Press
P.O. Box 8067
New Orleans, La. 70182

There are magazines that publish plays for young people:

Plays, The Drama Magazine for Young People
8 Arlington St.
Boston, Mass. 02116

Scholastic Magazines, Inc. (publishes plays occasionally)
50 W. 44th St.
New York, N.Y. 10036

For a more complete list of play publishers, see the "Sources of Materials."

Bookstores frequently have a section of drama books. You can find single plays as well as collections of plays in book form in that section.

The Drama Book Shop at 723 Seventh Avenue in New York City claims the largest selection of theater/drama books in the country. If you're ever in New York City, it's worth your time to stop in at the Drama Book Shop and take a look. They have books on every phase of theater, film, and TV as well as the most extensive collection of plays.

There may be a bookstore in your area that specializes in plays and drama books. The easiest way to find out is to check the bookstores listed in the telephone book. If you don't see a display ad, call one or two stores. They'll know which one carries the largest selection of drama books.

"But I'd rather see plays than read them!" lamented a student actress.

"That's the best way," her director agreed, "but that's not always possible. The next best way is to read them."

Many people enjoy reading plays as much as they do short stories or novels. Although plays don't tell you what characters are thinking (as novels do), plays do give stage directions for actions, sound effects, light cues, etc. Once you learn how to read a play, you'll see everything in your imagination as it happens.

Plays are fun to read out loud, by yourself or with a friend or two. In fact, there are many social groups that do just that. They get together for an evening and read aloud plays suggested by their members.

Look over a play script to get used to the format. The character's name is given first, then the speech (dialogue). All stage directions and actions are written in italics. For example:

GEORGE: I love you, Matilda.
MATILDA: Do you mean that?
(*They embrace*)

Encourage your group to read several plays aloud to help you make the choice for play production. It's a good way to get everyone involved in the play from the very beginning. The more plays you read, the more you'll have to choose from.

Chapter **6**

All About Musicals

"Music, music, music" is the lyric of an old popular song. There's something about a musical that has special appeal for most people. Part of the fun of doing a musical is humming the tunes for months, sometimes years, afterwards. Every time you hear the overture it will bring back memories. Everyone gets caught up with the rhythm and the melody of a musical.

Musicals are of two types: musical comedies and musical plays. Musical comedies focus on musical entertainment with less emphasis on the book. Generally speaking, musical comedies are easier to do than musical plays. Lyrics and music have a light, jaunty air about them. The father of musical comedy, a uniquely American form, is George M. Cohan. Cohan wrote musicals about patriotic subjects in the early 1900s.

A large space with a piano is needed for rehearsals of a musical.

An important part of casting is usually to have the actor read the part from the script.

A musical comedy like *Hello, Dolly* doesn't take the same amount of work that *West Side Story,* a musical play, does. (*West Side Story* is a modern version of *Romeo and Juliet,* a play by William Shakespeare.) Where musical comedy is frivolity and entertainment, the musical play is an art form concerned with ideas and human values. *West Side Story* grapples with grim social problems of everyday life. Every element of the production—music, songs, dance, and book—contributes to its searching point of view.

Musicals are not necessarily better or worse than straight plays. They are different. They demand a variety of skills.

Once you understand these differences, you will be better equipped to make a choice. Both types of plays offer some similar problems, as well as some specific for each.

"I'll never forget the first time I danced in a chorus line," a young player said with a grimace. "The lead girl started off with the wrong foot and threw off the whole line. It was a mess."

"Just be glad it wasn't you," her friend said.

"But it was," she answered. "I did keep smiling the whole time though. At least I remembered that."

Musicals require additional time and personnel, but can

generate a great deal of enthusiasm. Let's take a look at these needs. This chapter will look at the varieties of musicals available. Then we will compare the musical and the straight play. There are variations within each category: length, degree of difficulty (both technically and physically), and acting and/or singing requirements.

Once again, a musical demands additional rehearsals and personnel. But there are some exceptions. A musical like *The Fantasticks* takes less work than a straight play like *The Skin of Our Teeth*. (One is short with few characters. The other is long with a great many characters.)

Here's a good thing to remember: "The more people you have in your play or musical—the more work it takes." The play with a large cast takes more direction, more rehearsal time, more costumes, more make-up, more of everything. The director has a harder job. He puts more people onstage at one time and moves them around so that their movements seem natural and create an interesting stage picture.

The next thing to consider is the length of the script. Some musicals are shorter than their full-length counterparts. There are musicals done without an intermission, which run about an hour and a half, like *Joseph and the Amazing Technicolor Dreamcoat*. Some straight plays like *Long Day's Journey Into Night* run about three hours.

When you consider a musical, ask yourself the following questions:

1. How many musical numbers are in the show?
2. How many songs (solos, duets, chorus numbers, etc.)?
3. How many dances?
4. How many people are involved in each number?
5. How many in the entire cast?

Plan a rehearsal schedule. List each of the numbers, what has to be done, and the people involved in each. Remember that your rehearsal pianist cannot rehearse with the singers and the dancers at the same time. Put the music on tape, so that you can work on more than one musical number at a time. Dancers can work in one room with the tape while the pianist works with the singers in another room. Plan your rehearsal schedule so there's plenty of time to work with each group separately. Put them together when they are ready.

As the stage director, you may have someone to assist you as the musical director. Make sure you and the musical director agree on the interpretation of the numbers. If the director decides to handle the musical direction himself, he can have a vocal coach to help with the songs. Frequently, in amateur theater, the pianist and vocal coach are the same person. Sometimes one person serves in all three capacities: musical director, pianist, and vocal coach.

The choreographer is the dance director. He or she creates the dances and teaches them to the dancers. The choreographer will rehearse them until they're ready to become part of the whole. If there are solos, he or she will choreograph them. One of the dancers may function as the choreographer or it may be the director who handles this job as well.

Dance adds a visual excitement to the performance. It can serve as an important element to forward the plot. A perfect example of this is the musical, *A Chorus Line.* The world of dance and dancers is what the show is all about.

"If I had to say any lines on the stage, I know I'd freeze," a dancer said. "But, I can stay on that stage and dance until I drop, and I never get nervous. I wonder why?"

All musical numbers must be choreographed. When you see a singer in a musical, he or she doesn't just stand and sing. He moves around and seems to flow with the song. His movements emphasize the words. That movement was carefully worked out and rehearsed with the choreographer. Although there are many separate parts to a musical, they must all appear to come naturally as part of the whole.

One of the most important considerations in doing a musical is the cost. There's no doubt that most musicals cost more to produce than straight plays. You rent the musical score as well as the book. Most royalties for musicals are negotiated. No set fee is listed in catalogs as it is for straight plays.

The royalty fee you pay depends on such things as the size of your house (auditorium), seating capacity, number of performances, type of group, ticket prices, and whether you require orchestration. Most publishers charge an amateur group a lowered royalty fee.

The Tams-Witmark Music Library, Inc. catalog (see p. 65) says, "We are the world's largest and most experienced company in supplying musicals to amateur and professional groups."

Tams-Witmark will provide all the material necessary to prepare the production on a flexible, rental basis. This material includes prompt books, conductor scores, dialogue parts, chorus parts, vocal parts, orchestrations, and often stage directions.

You can send for reading copies of musicals published by Samuel French. You pay the postage plus a returnable deposit. For musicals published by Tams-Witmark Music Library, Inc., you pay postage only.

A spokesman for Tams-Witmark lists the dozen most popular musicals for the high-school market:

1. *You're a Good Man, Charlie Brown*
2. *Bye Bye Birdie*
3. *Mame*
4. *Finian's Rainbow*
5. *Li'l Abner*
6. *Hello, Dolly*
7. *Oliver*
8. *Anything Goes*
9. *Brigadoon*
10. *Camelot*
11. *The Wizard of Oz*
12. *Kiss Me, Kate*

There are some small-cast, simple-set musicals like *You're a Good Man, Charlie Brown; The Fantasticks;* and *By Strouse.* These can be done on a fairly small budget.

Even though musicals take more rehearsal time, many of the numbers can be rehearsed individually and at home. This is an advantage over most straight plays. Actors in straight plays cannot rehearse by themselves. Very few scenes are played with only one person. Straight plays take more interaction, so most actors are needed at every rehearsal.

Cast albums of some musicals are also available. Your group can listen and hear what the show should sound like.

"Our director won't let us listen to the record until we're ready to open. He doesn't want to show us up, I guess," a young singer said.

Many musical productions are done now with stereo tapes rather than live music. That means the music cues are the responsibility of the stage manager or the sound person, rather than the musical director or the accompanist.

It is possible to record your own music on tape. Most

performers prefer the excitement of live music and feel more secure with an accompanist who will follow them.

"What if you have to clear your throat or cough or something? The tape won't wait. I hate to work with tape," the singer said.

Those choices come later. Your first decision is which to try first—a musical or a straight play. Sooner or later, you'll do both.

How do some people who have tried both feel about it? One high-school actress summed up her feelings this way:

"I'm a singer, so, of course, I like musicals better. I feel more secure in doing what I know best."

Another equally talented young actor said, "Musicals are too messy for me. There are so many things to remember. I get too nervous. Give me a good comedy any time. Now that's really fun."

A director who does both musicals and straight plays explained it this way: "It really depends on your group. If everyone in the cast can carry a tune, move fairly well, and is willing to work hard, then I'll do a musical with them. *But*—" he emphasized the word, "*But* if they don't want to put in the time and the effort, they're better off with a straight play with just enough roles for the ones who will work."

"Both are fun. I like to do a good drama, a comedy, and a musical. Why stick to one thing?" says another experienced director. "I love it all!"

Before you make your decision to do a straight play or a musical, consider the following:

1. Size of cast
2. Length of show
3. Degree of difficulty (Is it a musical comedy or a musical play?)

4. How many special numbers (solos, duets, chorus, dances, etc.)?
5. Roles needed (Can you cast it?)
6. Budget (Can you afford it?)
7. Rehearsal time (Do you have enough time to put it together and do it well?)

And, don't forget the first rule you learned in choosing any show: It must be a play you like—a play that excites you.

Chapter 7

What It Takes to Be a Director

Someone once said, "The director is like a traffic cop. He tells you when to stop and when to go."

That definition of a director's duties is far too simple, of course, but essentially the director does map out the flow of traffic onstage. He or she blocks the action: that means deciding on the entrances, exits, crosses, and all other movements of the actors on stage.

The director is the one who brings all the elements of the show together. The director decides which values of the play to emphasize. This person must have an eye for every aspect of the production. The director is reponsible for putting all the separate pieces of the puzzle together so that the audience can recognize the picture. Does it sound like a big job? *It is.*

One director likes to repeat this line: "When the play is good, everyone says the *actors* did a great job. But when it's terrible, they say what a rotten job the *director* did."

The director has more responsibilities than anyone else.

It's a good idea to find a director with some experience in putting on plays or in acting in them, if possible.

You may find yourself directing the play. Where do you start?

Let's say you've chosen the play and are excited about it. Before you do anything else, read the script again. Try to visualize the actions. Make some notes for yourself. How do you see this scene? What is the character's action at this moment? What kind of person should play the part? What qualities will you look for in the actor to play each role?

You may change your mind several times about how you want a scene played. That's fine. Don't be afraid to make changes. But begin with an overall approach to the play. Give some thought to what the play has to say. Where is the climax or high point of action?

Right about now, *stop!* Ask yourself if you *like* the play. Remember that you are going to live with the play for a long time. In a good play, you can find something new each time you read it or see it.

Some Broadway actors play the same part for years. How do they keep from getting bored? One actor said, "I must find something new every night."

THE DIRECTOR'S CONCEPT

After you have read the play several times, plan how you will direct it. Your idea or concept of how the play should be done is called the *directorial concept.* Before you cast your play, think about your production elements. Make sure the actors, scenery, music, costumes, and props all contribute to one *idea.*

What kind of set will you need? Can you do the play

with curtains only or on a bare stage? Does the play need costumes? Does it call for special props or difficult technical effects? Most directors would love to do *Peter Pan,* but few can afford the flying machine for Peter and the children to fly on the stage. That is a special technical effect, an important one to that play.

Most beginning directors would choose a different play unless they had a large budget and a lot of experienced help. Give some thought to the kind of play most appropriate for your particular audience, theater, or space.

Start a checklist for yourself. Jot down everything you plan for each area of your production. You may change your mind but you'll have some ideas written down for future reference. Don't try to remember everything. You may forget one of your most exciting first images about the play.

CASTING

Casting a play is a problem for even the most experienced directors. Professional directors usually cast actors whose work they know and/or actors they've worked with before. For a beginning director this is rarely possible. You may know how someone behaves in class or at a party, but when that same person is on the stage, he may become self-conscious and tense.

"A play is easy to direct if you cast it well," said one director. She advised, "Cast the best actors, the ones who look right."

Consider the visual first. Never cast someone just because he or she is a friend. Choose the right type. At the same time, keep your mind open. Just because the description of a character says he is tall or short, you don't have to go with that. Those are the things you can change.

Never rush your casting. Hold your tryouts over several days if possible. Try to see your would-be-actors in as many different situations as possible. They behave one way when they're happy and quite another when they are angry or upset. You need to see them in several different emotional situations.

TRYOUT METHODS

The most popular method of tryouts is to have your actors read several scenes from the script. Ask your actors to read for a few different parts—even parts you're not considering them for. Choose the scenes to read ahead of time. Go through the play and pick out those scenes that give a good indication of the role. Pick scenes which show different sides of the character.

You will need to find a few scenes for each character. Find scenes that show different moods and emotions. You will want scenes with different characters together. It is important to see how different characters react to each other. You must look for contrasts in character, personality, voice, and physical types.

After you have heard your actors read a variety of roles, ask them to put down their scripts. Let them try an improvisation. (Improvisation is spontaneous dialogue and action made up on the spot.) Begin with an improvisation on one of the scenes in the script. Ask them to play it in their own words. You may prefer to give them a specific improvisation to act out. (See Chapter 9.) Ask for an improvisation that will show a quality or emotion you are looking for.

A pantomime exercise is an easy way to get your actors moving. Give them a specific task, which involves moving an imaginary object or person from one side of the stage to the other. Give them imaginary obstacles to go around or over. You might ask an actor to pick up a large dog and carry him to the other side and give him a bath. This will give you an idea of the actor's physical flexibility and imagination.

It is important to see your actors move. A beautiful girl who clomps across the stage like an elephant will not be convincing as a fairy princess. Everyone has a specific quality. You are looking for a certain quality in each of your characters.

In a well-directed scene all the important action can be seen and heard.

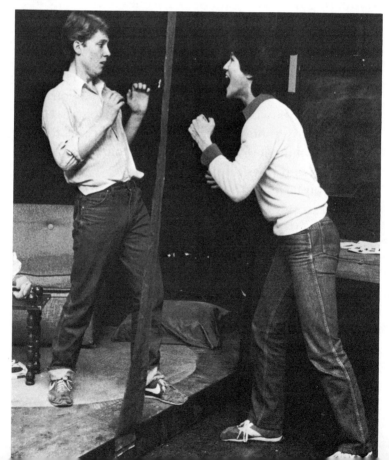

Another consideration will be how your whole cast looks together. If you are casting a play that requires two different families, as in *Abie's Irish Rose,* you can't cast all blondes or all brunettes. You want actors who look different from each other and are easily identifiable.

There are times when two people are equally well suited for a part. Again, you have to consider the balance of your cast. You must have a variety of types.

Make sure you have everyone onstage or in the acting space together at one time. That way you can tell how they will look in the stage picture. If you cast an actor who is five and a half feet as a father and a six-foot son, generally it will not be believable. Keep physical relationships in mind when you cast.

If possible, hold your tryouts in the auditorium or space where the play will be presented. You can check vocal quality and voice projection for that area.

"I'll never forget the time we did a show for senior citizens in a retirement home," a young director said. "One old man walked right up to the foot of the stage and shouted at the actor. 'Louder, Sonny,' he said. That actor learned a lesson he never forgot."

An actor's voice is very important. It is equally as important as his physical type. Look for variety and flexibility, as well as good diction. You will not have time to correct sloppy speech habits during rehearsals.

MUSICAL AUDITIONS

When you do a musical, you need a separate tryout for songs and dances. You can ask for a prepared song and/or dance. And ask for one of the songs in the show also.

Have an accompanist at the audition as well. Each actor must bring music for his song so the accompanist can play it.

What do you do if you have a good actor who doesn't sing too well or a terrific singer who doesn't act too well? There are two schools of thought on this quandary. It would depend on the importance of the music. Some directors would go with the singer and spend extra time working on his acting. Another director would prefer the actor and spend extra time on singing. It's a tossup.

Always hold "call backs" after two or three open auditions. Call back those actors that you are most interested in. Find out if they are willing to accept any role in the play—not just the lead. When you ask people to come back for several tryout sessions, you get an idea of their interest. And you can tell if there's improvement with each reading of the script.

Some actors are poor "cold readers." That means they do not perform well at first readings. Other actors are exceptionally good. Sometimes the good readers never develop beyond the first reading, while the first reader that begins badly continues to improve right up to the performance.

Be on the lookout for the actor who seems sincere and willing to work. If he has energy and a good imagination he may be better for your play than the actor who reads exceptionally well.

At your call backs, make sure everyone understands the commitment of doing a play. If possible, have your rehearsal schedule ready so each person can see the time that is expected. Ask everyone to look carefully at the rehearsal schedule and production dates. Make sure there are no conflicts. Actors may have to miss one or two rehearsals. Most directors will work around that as long as they know beforehand. No actor is ever excused from final dress rehearsals or technical rehearsals.

Picking your cast is always a calculated risk. What's best for the play and the entire production must always come first. This can be a hard rule to remember when you are working with a group of friends.

BLOCKING

When you read the play, you imagine what happens as each action takes place. You probably have a picture in your mind, like a movie. That's how directors read a play for the first time. Whether you're an experienced director or a beginner, you must visualize how the action should look on stage.

After you have made notes and seen the play in your mind's eye, you can write out specific blocking for certain scenes.

Start with your stage diagram. As we have mentioned, stage directions are given from the actor's point of view. When he stands on the stage facing the audience, his left is SL (stage left) and his right is SR (stage right). US means upstage, away from the audience. DS is downstage, toward the audience.

Think about the stage you will use. If it's an auditorium, with a raised platform in the front of the room, you can block in the traditional manner. Use the symbols for stage areas given above.

If you work in the round, you will have to make some adjustments. If you are playing in the middle of a large room or with the audience seated on three or four sides, you will have some different problems. The most important thing to remember is that the audience must see and hear the actors. As long as you remember that, you will solve whatever problems occur.

When you play in the round, make sure the audience sees the face of at least one of your actors at all times. Move your actors in such a way that the audience sees all the players some of the time and at least one all of the time.

Some directors block the whole play in their heads and write out the directions in their play book before rehearsals begin. Others like to work with models of the set and move around little dolls (or sticks to represent the actors) to various positions on the set. That way they know where each of their characters is at any given time. It's easy to forget the character in the room who hasn't spoken for two pages.

By now, you've guessed that there are as many different ways to block a show as there are directors. Most directors change and simplify blocking in later rehearsals as the actors discover better ways of moving and reacting. There are some directors who like to improvise with their actors before they begin blocking.

A smart beginner will have his or her blocking ideas worked out and written in the prompt book. He or she will be open to suggestion, however, especially if an actor has a strong inclination to move in a specific direction. Most directors will say, "Go with it."

Encourage your actors to experiment if they can. Most inexperienced actors need to be told exactly when and where to move. They feel more secure with this kind of direction.

When you prepare your blocking, remember that each scene has an action. Work out the blocking so that the action of the scene is clear. Keep in mind that a standing character will dominate one that is sitting. The actor who is turned more toward the front will be stronger than the one whose face and body is partly turned away from the audience. The attention of the audience will be directed toward the actor that other actors are looking at.

Remember the importance of contrast. If you have three guards standing at attention on one side of the stage, the person seated on the rock on the other side will get the attention.

You can show relationships through blocking. One of the hardest things for young inexperienced actors to do onstage is embrace. Somehow their body positions end up looking like a pyramid.

Movement can be more important than words. If an actor said, "I can't stand you!" and came very close to the other person and stroked his arm, what would you think? You wouldn't believe it. But if he turned his back on the other character and said it you would believe it.

Actors are rarely onstage alone, and then it's only for a short time. Each actor must be aware of others onstage.

A long talky scene will need to be broken up with action. As the scene progresses, movement will be added to reinforce the action of the scene.

Draw a floor plan with your set indicated. Draw all the entrances and exits (which may be the same) and the furniture on stage. Plan your blocking with this floor plan in mind. The actors follow curved paths around the furniture to give a sense of depth to the stage.

DIRECTORIAL APPROACH

Some directors approach a play as a dictator. They want their actors to perform like puppets. Other directors like to experiment with many different ideas before they decide on specific blocking for a scene. The director must know what he or she wants to happen in each scene even if he's not exactly sure of how he wants to get there.

Remember that the important actions of the play must be seen. Don't place an important action USL (upstage left) behind a chair. Bring it downstage where your audience can see—"open it up."

A large part of the play's blocking will be obvious. When

A page of an actor's typed play script with blocking written in.

XC with Prudence

QUAKER
There's nothin' else to do here.

PRUDENCE
He's not been a Quaker long, William. He'll learn.

WM. PENN
(GENTLY) Well...did thee play?

QUAKER
(SIGHS) I did.

hangs head

WM. PENN
Then thee will have to be punished.

QUAKER   *Run L. around*
(RUNNING TO HIDE BEHIND HER)
Punished?

WM. PENN
(KINDLY) If he doesn't know our rules, Prudence, thee had better teach him.
(WM. PENN SITS KEG STAGE L.)

PRUDENCE
(THE TEACHER) All offenses against God, such as drunkeness, cursing, lying,
duels, murder, profane language, stage plays... (SHE STOPS MOMENTARILY, AS
ALL OF THE ACTORS REACT. THEN, SHE LOOKS AT THE AUDIENCE, DOES A TAKE, AND
GETS BACK INTO THE SCENE.) Cards, dice, and gambling---are to be punished

WM. PENN
(KINDLY) Since it's his first time, let him pray for forgiveness at the
meeting today.

QUAKER
XR (RUSHING OVER TO WM. PENN AND SHAKING HIS HANDS) Oh, I thank thee. I'll
pray real hard.
(HE DASHES OFF.) *→ exit S. L.*

PRUDENCE
(STEPPING DOWN TO AUDIENCE) And I'll see that he does.   (EXIT)

JOSHUA
(SIGHS) You're too easy on them, sir. I'd tan his hide to make sure he
remembers.

WM. PENN
It's for him to instruct his own conscience.

one character must strike another, if he is on the other side of the stage he will have to cross (X) to do it. Some of the blocking is written in the script. Use it as a suggestion, but don't feel you must stick to it. The position of entrances and exits may be different on your stage. That would change the blocking drastically.

For example, if the play calls for an actor to enter DSR (downstage right) but your entrance is USC (upstage center), you can see how much that would change the blocking indicated in the script.

REHEARSALS

The first rehearsal is very important. It will set the tone for the rehearsal period. Make your expectations known from the beginning. Your first rehearsal will be a read through of the entire play. Many directors prefer several read through rehearsals before they begin blocking. They discuss the play and what it says. The director encourages the actors to talk about their characters, to talk about their relationships to each other and to the whole play.

Devote plenty of time for each blocking rehearsal. You will need at least one two- or three-hour rehearsal for each act. As you block each act, the stage manager will write the blocking in the prompt book.

To refresh your memory of what the prompt book looks like, see page 20.

Each actor will write blocking in his script. All blocking is written in pencil. There will be changes. There always are.

Once you block the first act, go back over it immediately. It's best to make sure everyone understands the specific blocking. Go over it again if necessary. Double check that everyone has it correctly. Do not begin blocking another act until everyone is sure of what has been done.

Careful blocking helps the actors to understand their characters and the entire play. This shows the actors that the director has done his advance planning—his homework. That always helps build confidence in the director. Most directors will allow actors to try additional things. But the director decides which blocking to discard and which to use.

As rehearsals progress and relationships develop, the actors may feel motivated to move to a different place or add some stage business. (He or she might pick up a book and look at it and put it down in another spot, take a piece of candy from a dish, pour a drink, etc.)

There are no short cuts to blocking. It must be done carefully and thoroughly. It is a time consuming business. But, careful preparation in the beginning will pay off.

LINES

After blocking rehearsals are finished, *then* lines are learned. It is easier to learn lines along with movement. Some directors allow paraphrasing of lines. But playwrights frown on this practice. It is important for an actor to give the same cue each time. Therefore, it is best to learn lines exactly, word for word whenever possible.

PROPS AND COSTUMES

After blocking and lines are learned, start to use hand props. Most play scripts have props listed in the back of the book. Some also list sound and lighting cues as well.

Begin sound cues soon after props. Don't fail into the trap of saying, "Bang" for a gun shot. Your actor may get so used to saying it, he'll do it in performance. Some actors get used to pantomiming props that are not available and are awkward when they finally get the real prop.

Costumes can help actors get into their parts. Many young actresses need practice with long skirts and certain types of shoes. High heels can be a positive menace for a young girl who isn't used to them. Get your actors out of their blue jeans and sneakers in plenty of time to be comfortable in their costumes.

"I just don't feel right in a suit," an actor may say.

You'd better get him in a suit and keep him in it for as many rehearsals as necessary for him to appear comfortable wearing it. The whole point of the costume is to help create his character. That character is comfortable in his clothes, even if he's in a leprechaun's outfit. The actor must be just as comfortable with the costume as the character would be.

When lines are learned and blocking secure, the director begins to polish the play. He tries to develop the rhythm and continuity of the play. He wants the play to be believable and to seem spontaneous, as if it's really happening for the first time!

TECHNICAL AND DRESS REHEARSAL

The technical rehearsal combines all the elements of light, props, sound, and any special effects. The scenery is in completed form at this time.

There will be new people backstage to handle the technical elements or the actors will be responsible for them. The stage manager is in charge of the backstage crew.

The technical rehearsal is for the benefit of the technical crew. Actors may be asked to repeat the same cue many times until the timing is perfect—until it is *technically* correct.

A community theater director told her group, "Nothing makes an amateur theater look better than a perfect technical production."

On the other hand, nothing calls attention to itself like a light going on or off at the wrong time. That's almost as bad as the telephone ringing after the actor picks it up.

Dress rehearsal should be a performance or as nearly like a performance as possible. No stops should be made for any reason. Everything should be at performance level.

"That's great advice," commented an experienced director. "But it's wishful thinking. I've yet to see a perfect dress rehearsal. Something always goes wrong."

"I remember the dress rehearsal on *Anastasia,*" an actress said. "I fell right through the couch. It came apart. It was hilarious."

"I had an experience once," another actor offered. "The only entrance door on stage left, where I entered, was stuck. And there was no crossover backstage. I had to run around the building outside in the freezing rain and enter from stage right. I was only a little late . . . and my teeth were chattering. I said some dumb thing about being all wet."

Some directors invite audiences to their dress rehearsals. This helps everyone to stay on their toes and makes it more like a performance. It also helps the actors get the feeling of working in front of an audience.

The better the dress rehearsal, the better the play will be. It has all the problems worked out. But don't worry. There are very few perfect dress rehearsals. That's probably why people fall back on that old cliché: "A bad dress rehearsal means a good opening night."

After the dress rehearsal, as with the preceding ones, the director gives notes (suggestions for improvement) to the cast and crew. Don't try to make any drastic changes at this late date. Encourage everyone. Help them feel confident with the show. But keep them reaching for a final performance.

Once the curtain goes up, the director's job is finished. He or she should sit in the audience and enjoy the show. It is now the stage manager's job to run the show, just as he or she has done from backstage for the last five or six rehearsals.

As you can see, directing isn't easy. It is the single hardest job in the theater. When you are the director, outline your goals for the play from the very beginning.

In addition to your directorial knowledge, you will need to be patient, fair, understanding, encouraging, and firm. And this above all: Keep your sense of humor.

The director sets the tone at the very first meeting of the cast. His or her dedication and concentration should be contagious. The director must respect the talent of the entire cast and crew and encourage them to respect each other. Every person associated with the play is important.

The Three Musketeers had the right idea: "All for one and one for all."

Chapter 8

Some Tips on Acting

Most people want to act. You'll have no trouble finding volunteers for that. We all act in our everyday lives. Every time you tell a story or relate an incident with action, you attempt to share your experience with someone else—the audience.

If you like to tell jokes and repeat them in a dramatic way, that also is a kind of acting. When you're bored in school, you have to look interested, so you *act* like you're interested.

Did a friend ever ask you if you liked her new dress? And you really didn't like it, but you didn't want to hurt your friend's feelings, so you said, "It's really nice." And you convinced yourself it was. Most of us do some acting in our everyday lives without even knowing it.

How can you make the transition from acting in life to acting onstage? It's easier for some people than for others. Almost every child is a good actor. Watch some young children at play when they are not aware of you. Their make believe can be as truthful and real as a great acting performance. But if they become aware of you or their audience, their behavior changes. They begin to show off or ham it up.

What causes this change in behavior? The youngsters lost their concentration on the game. They stopped concentrating on their make-believe action. They suddenly became aware of you and themselves.

There are hundreds of books about acting. There are more definitions of the word than you'd care to count. For our purposes, let's use a very simple one: "Acting is believing with your whole self and communicating that belief to an audience."

The actor is the one onstage, the one the audience sees. He represents not only himself but the playwright, the director, and everyone else who works on the production. The actor is the one element of a play you cannot do without.

Stanislavsky, the great director of the Moscow Art Theater, wrote in his book, *My Life In Art:* "The theater exists above all, for the actor, and without him, it cannot exist at all."

THE ACTOR'S INSTRUMENT

Every artist uses tools. The painter has canvas and brushes. The musician has an instrument and the score. The actor also has an instrument. That instrument must be tuned like a fine piano or violin. The actor's instrument consists of: body, voice, emotions, and imagination. The actor must tune his instrument just like the violinist. He must exercise just as the pianist practices scales.

Begin each rehearsal with body exercises. Start with exercises that stretch the muscles and relax them. Create a sequence of warm-ups for yourself. Most professional actors do their warm-ups before every rehearsal and performance. The warm-up not only prepares the body for work and keeps it flexible, but it also helps clear the mind.

One director said these physical warm-ups "erase the blackboard of the mind."

Remember that these exercises should relax the body and release tension. Calisthenics are not necessary. Simple stretching, neck rolls, swinging, and bouncing activities are best. Animal stretches are fun. Think of your favorite animal waking up in the morning. Stretch as that animal would. Work on every part of your body.

PANTOMIME

Pantomime is a good exercise for the body and the imagination. They work together in pantomime. Here are several pantomime activities for beginners. Think of others to add to this list.

1. Go through your morning routine at the sink. (Wash your face, brush your teeth, etc.)
2. Dress for the day.
3. Choose a fruit from a large basket. Prepare it and eat it.
4. Pick up a small animal.
5. Move a large object. (Do this alone and then with a partner.)

Remember, in pantomime, you must visualize fully what you see before you begin the action. Ask yourself some questions about the object for pantomime. Think about the shape, weight, texture, color, and smell (if any). Try to make it as real for yourself as possible.

Actors tune their bodies like musical instruments through a series of warm-ups.

Pantomime is a good way to exercise the body and the mind through total concentration.

Show your pantomime to a friend. If it is specific enough, your friend will guess what you're doing with no difficulty.

THE VOICE

One thing is certain. An actor must speak clearly and distinctly. He or she must be heard. The performance can be perfect, but if the audience can't hear the words, they won't care about the performance.

There is a famous speech in Shakespeare's *Hamlet.* Hamlet gives advice to the actors within the play. He says:

Speak the speech, I pray you, as I pronounced it to you, trippingly on the tongue. But if you mouth it, as many of our players do, I had as lief the town-crier spoke my lines. Nor do not saw the air too much with your hand, thus, but use all gently, for in the very torrent, tempest, and (as I may say) the whirlwind of passion, you must acquire and begat a temperance that may give it smoothness. O, it offends me to the soul to hear a robustious periwig-pated fellow tear a passion to tatters, to very rags, to split the ears of the groundlings . . .

Hamlet, ACT III, Sc. 2

Not only is this good advice, it is a good practice piece to read aloud. It calls for good diction and breath control.

Here's a good breathing exercise. Bend over from the waist and exhale—push out all your air. Breathe in slowly as you straighten up. Then count out loud from one to five. Project fully with each number. Try again and count to ten.

Here are some tongue twisters to practice. Don't try to say them fast. Try to say each one clearly and distinctly. These are good to keep on the dressing-room wall and practice before each performance.

1. Around the rugged rock, the ragged rascal ran.
2. Didn't Danny drive downtown?
3. Healthy Hannah had heavy hips.
4. Pretty Penny planted plenty.
5. Six silly sailors set sail on the seven seas.
6. Tip of the tongue, top of the teeth.
7. Rubber baby buggy bumpers.
8. Abraham asked Aaron about Amos.
9. She sells seashells by the seashore.
10. Make mine milk, mother.

Stanislavsky told his actors: "To an actor a word is not just a sound, it is the evocation of images. Your job is to instill your inner visions in others . . . and convey it in words."

BUILDING A CHARACTER

The Senses

How many of us use our five senses to their fullest? It is the rare person who does. Most of us depend heavily on sight. Some of us have a keen sense of hearing. Others have a strong sense of smell or taste. All of us are aware of touch, but not all of us have sharpened that sense to its finest point.

The five senses are a great asset to the actor. Everyone can benefit from increased sensory awareness, both in the theater and out.

Your senses can help stimulate your imagination and emotions—and vice versa. The stimulus can come from either direction. Here are some exercises for sensory awareness. Don't be surprised when your emotions come into play. You will see how closely aligned the senses are to the emotions.

1. Describe, in as much detail as possible, someone you dislike or someone who makes you angry. (sight)
2. Hear a strange noise in your house when you know no one else is home. (sound)
3. Smell smoke in the baby's room where you are babysitting. (smell)
4. Your best friend baked a beautiful chocolate cake for your birthday, but it tastes terrible. (taste)
5. Touch a soft, furry kitten. (touch)

In these exercises, you stimulated your sensory awareness and used your imagination to create an emotional reaction.

Concentration

If there is one thing of utmost importance for the actor, it's concentration. An actor must "stay with it." That means he must stay in his part, in character, every moment. He must not "break"—come out of the part. (Frequently, a "break" comes from something funny. The actor allows it to reach him inside the character.)

You'll hear an actor say, "I lost it!" which means he lost his concentration. He let something distract him momentarily.

One young actress had the classic accident onstage. Her

skirt fell off. Without missing a beat, she stepped out of it, picked it up and ad-libbed, "Keep them amused until I return." The other actors broke up, but she didn't.

On the stage, you must live the reality of your role from moment to moment. You cannot allow your concentration to falter for even an instant. Don't jump ahead in your mind to think about your next line. You must live each moment as it happens.

There are ways to practice and improve concentration. A good way is to imagine an image like a white candle on a black background. Close your eyes and try to create that picture in your mind. The hard part is to hold that image. You must keep working on the details every second. Is it short or tall? Is it thick? Is it off-white or pure white? Is it smooth? Is it lit? What is the background?

Try this exercise several times until you can hold your image for a minute or two. You cannot allow another thought to enter your mind or you will lose the image.

Try other images for yourself once you have learned the technique.

Essentials

The three essential ingredients for good acting are the same essential ingredients for good living:

1. Be in touch with yourself.
2. Be in touch with others.
3. Be in touch with your environment.

The great actress Laurette Taylor, who created the part of Amanda in *The Glass Menagerie* by Tennessee Williams, was asked what the secret of her great acting was. She answered the question this way: "Did you ever play house?"

Chapter 9

Improvisations for Acting

Improvisation is spontaneous, spur-of-the-moment acting without a script. The players make up their own dialogue as they go.

We improvise all the time in our own lives. Sometimes we do this easily and say exactly the right thing. Other times we are at a loss for words. Whatever the response, it is spontaneous and unrehearsed.

Improvisation is used for many purposes in addition to actor training. It is the basis of role play used in a variety of therapeutic ways. Improvisation is a training technique used for salesmen, personnel counselors, teachers, etc. One group called Performing Arts for Crises Training (PART) uses improvisations for training policemen, social workers, hospital personnel, etc. This group creates the crisis situations and the outsiders or trainees (policemen, group workers, etc.) are called into the unknown crisis situation and must deal with the problems they meet. Sometimes it's a family dispute between a husband and wife or father and son. The trainee comes into the improvisation in the middle of the excitement. He or she must improvise a way to handle the situation.

Two high-school actresses have an amusing way to practice improvisation. They stand in a crowded elevator of the local department store. One girl begins telling the other some outlandish tale in hushed tones, but loud enough to be overheard by the other passengers. Just as she reaches the climactic point . . . "and then she saw what it really was—"

"Four, please," the other girl interrupts.

The girls know their improvisation succeeds when someone in the elevator asks, "Well, what did she see?"

Stories, scenes from plays, and characters can be the basis for improvisations. You can make up an improvisation by using an object such as a wallet or a piece of drift wood. You can build an improvisation from a costume or a hat. You can even do an improvisation based on nothing more than a word or a line of dialogue.

It's easier to begin improvisations from a specific story or situation. Sometimes it's hard to think of what to say next. But the more you practice, the easier it is.

One thing to remember in improvisation is to listen to the other person. Acting is also *reacting*.

Here are some scenes to complete. You improvise the ending. Read the script to the point where it stops. Then make up your own dialogue. Sometimes you will create a satisfying ending. Other times you will ramble on. Stop the improvisation when you feel it is finished or it isn't going anywhere.

HOMEWORK

(THE SCENE TAKES PLACE IN A KITCHEN. MOTHER IS PREPARING FOOD. DAUGHTER IS SEATED READING A MAGAZINE.)

MOTHER: (LOOKS AT DAUGHTER) I thought you had homework. That doesn't look like homework to me.

DAUGHTER: (STILL READING) Eh-huh.

MOTHER: Peel these potatoes. There's too much to do around here to waste time reading that trash.

DAUGHTER: Aw, come on, mom. Can't you see I'm busy?

MOTHER: Busy! You call that busy? I can't do everything around here myself.

DAUGHTER: (STILL LOOKING AT MAGAZINE) Wait until I finish this.

MOTHER: I need your help . . . *now.*

DAUGHTER: I have to do my homework first.

MOTHER: You can peel the potatoes first.

DAUGHTER: Aw, come on, mom.

MOTHER: You heard me.

DAUGHTER: In a minute.

MOTHER: *Now!*

DAUGHTER: Leave me alone.

MOTHER: I said *now!* You never do anything around here. You're always goofing off!

DAUGHTER: . . . .

You're probably feeling something by now no matter which role you're playing. You may say things out of anger or frustration. See if you can solve the problem some way. Your solution may be to walk out or it might be to peel the potatoes. You may come up with another action. When you feel the problem has been solved or that you can go no further, say "Stop."

Talk about what happened after you left the script. What were some of the good things that occurred? What were some of the good lines that came out?

Read it again. Switch roles. Continue from where the printed play stops. Make up your own words. When you finish, discuss how this was different from the first time. Which improvisation had more drama? Why?

Try the next one. Although this is written for a father and son, it can be done with several combinations. Father and daughter, mother and son, or mother and daughter.

THE BANQUET

(THE SCENE TAKES PLACE IN THE LIVING ROOM. SON IS COMBING HIS HAIR, GETTING READY TO GO OUT. HE LOOKS AT THE CLOCK. FATHER ENTERS.)

SON: Hi, dad. I was getting worried.

FATHER: Worried? Worried about what?

SON: I don't want to be late.

FATHER: Late for what?

SON: The father and son banquet. You know . . . for the basketball team.

FATHER: Oh . . . yeah. I guess I forgot.

SON: (DISAPPOINTED) Forgot! That's all right. I got the tickets. You have time to change.

FATHER: Yeah, well . . . you see . . .

SON: What's the matter?

FATHER: I forgot.

SON: There's time.

FATHER: No. I can't go. I told the boss I'd come back to work tonight. I'm sorry, I forgot.

SON: But I got the tickets.

FATHER: Yeah, well, I already told him I'd work. It's time and a half. There'll be another dinner.

SON: I'm getting an award tonight.

FATHER: Maybe you can sell my ticket. (SIGHS) Look, kid, I've got other things to do. What can I tell you!

SON: . . . .

Continue the improvisation from here. Take it any way your feelings direct. When you have gone as far as you can or want to, say, "Stop."

Talk about the improvisation. What were some of the feelings that occurred? Did your emotions get involved? How did they change? Did you feel guilt, anger, sadness?

How did you deal with those feelings with your dialogue? Reverse roles and try the scene again. Discuss the differences in the improvisations. Which was more believable? Why? Which was more dramatic? Why?

Improvise the next two scenes.

BREAK UP

This improvisation is for a young man and woman.

(THE SCENE TAKES PLACE IN OR AROUND SCHOOL.)

HE: (CHEERFULLY) Hi. Where have you been? I haven't seen you all day.

SHE: Yeah, I know. I've been busy.

HE: Too busy for me?

SHE: No, not exactly.

HE: What's that mean, "not exactly"?

SHE: There's something we have to talk about.

HE: It sounds serious.

SHE: It is.

HE: What happened? Did you flunk the final?

SHE: No, I don't think so.

HE: Then what's the matter?

SHE: It's about us.

HE: About us? What about us?

SHE: I don't know how to say this exactly, but—

HE: But what? What's the matter with you? You've been acting kind of strange all week.

SHE: Well, that's what I want to talk about. (TAKES A DEEP BREATH) I don't think we should see each other anymore.

HE: Not see each other? What are you talking about? We've been going together for almost a year.

SHE: . . . .

Keep it going from here until you reach some conclusion or want to say, "Stop."

What did it feel like to be rejected? What did it feel like to reject someone? Be sure to play this scene again and

Improvisation is a good exercise for an actor whether it is done alone or with a group.

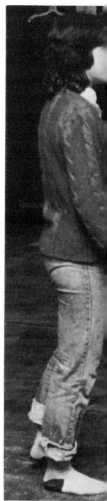

reverse the roles. Talk about this improvisation and discuss other ways it could have gone. Was it dramatic? How could it have been more so?

By now, you're getting the idea. You can take your improvisations in a variety of directions. Here's the last one. See how you will solve this problem.

THE BRACELET

(THE SCENE TAKES PLACE IN A DEPARTMENT STORE. JANE AND EVELYN ARE ADMIRING THE BRACELETS ON THE JEWELRY COUNTER, WHEN JANE SLIPS ONE OF THE BRACELETS IN HER BAG.)

EVELYN: (IN SURPRISE) Jane!

JANE: What's the matter?

EVELYN: You know what's the matter. (INDICATING HER BAG)

JANE: Nobody saw me.

EVELYN: *I* saw you.

JANE: What are you going to do—turn me in?

EVELYN: Put it back.

JANE: No. (SHE WALKS TO THE NEXT COUNTER)

EVELYN: (FOLLOWS HER) Jane, put that bracelet back or you'll get in trouble.

JANE: What trouble? Nobody saw me. (SHE LOOKS AROUND) Just act natural.

EVELYN: How can I act natural? I'm scared!

JANE: What's there to be scared of? Come on, let's go.

EVELYN: (TAKING JANE'S ARM) Put the bracelet back, Jane. Please.

JANE: Why should I?

EVELYN: It's *stealing*.

JANE: They'll never miss it. Come on. (STARTS TO GO)

EVELYN: Wait, I . . .

JANE: You're chicken. That's what you are, *chicken*.

EVELYN: I am not. I just don't like stealing, that's all.

JANE: Come on, here comes someone.

(STORE DETECTIVE ENTERS)

DETECTIVE: Just a minute, girls—

Finish the scene in your own words.

Drama is conflict. Each of these improvisations has a problem or conflict already set up. The first part of the script will help you to get into character to continue the improvisation as that character.

After you feel confident with these improvisations, you're ready to make up the whole thing. It's best to start with two- or three-person improvisations until you get used to the give and take of spontaneous dialogue. The following improvisations offer conflicts or problems. Begin from there.

cop. 2

SIMPLE SITUATION IMPROVISATIONS

1. You need to borrow $20 from your best friend. (You haven't paid him/her back from the last time you borrowed money.)
2. Try to convince a teacher to change your grade. (The teacher doesn't believe in changing grades.)
3. Try to borrow class notes from the "brain" in class. (The "brain" doesn't lend notes to anyone.)
4. You're invited to a big dance on Saturday night, but you already have a babysitting job. Convince your sister to take your place. (She doesn't like kids.)
5. Try to borrow your best friend's new dress (or sports coat). (You spilled ketchup on the last one you borrowed.)
6. Return an item to a department store. (The clerk says you didn't buy the item there.)
7. You are waiting for a bus and discover you lost your wallet. Try to borrow money from a stranger. (He thinks all kids are out to take advantage of him.)
8. Convince the librarian that you must take out a reference book overnight. (The library does not allow reference books to go out.)
9. Your date wants to go to a place that your parents disapprove of. (He has already made the reservations.)
10. You and your friend find a purse with $50 in it and a card with the owner's name. You want to return it. (Your friend wants to keep the money.)

There's no right or wrong when you do an improvisation. It can turn out many different ways. One thing that's important is to stay in character until you finish the improvisation or stop it.

Some people will find improvisations easy, while others will not. Many fine actors are not good at improvisations. Yet some are so skilled they can improvise before an audience and always entertain.

With practice most people enjoy doing improvisations. It's a good way to create scenes. It's good practice for an actor. And it is a valuable playwriting technique.

STORY IMPROVISATIONS

For story improvisations, choose a story that the group knows and is familiar with. Tell the story first. Discuss the plot and dramatic elements. Ask each person to choose a character and describe that character. When everyone seems sure of their character and the action, improvise the story. Discuss it when you're finished and try it again. Switch parts to get a different point of view.

Fairy tales, folk tales, fables, and myths are good sources for stories to improvise. Some that work particularly well are:

1. The Elves and the Shoemaker
2. The Frog Prince
3. King Midas and the Golden Touch
4. Androcles and the Lion
5. The Tortoise and the Hare
6. The Town Mouse and the City Mouse
7. Rumplestiltskin
8. The Boy Who Cried Wolf
9. Robin Hood
10. A Christmas Carol

GROUP IMPROVISATIONS

Group improvisations are good ways to get several people involved. With four or five people faced with the same problem, the burden on each individual is lessened. When you do group improvisations, decide who you are first.

Here are several group improvisations for five people. You will get the idea after you try these. Then you can make up more for yourself.

1. You are one of five people marooned on a desert island. One person discovers a rowboat which will hold four people. Decide who will go and who will stay.
2. You are trapped in an underground mine. One of you must try to crawl through the nearly collapsed tunnel to get help. Decide who will go.
3. You are on a sinking ship. There is a lifeboat ready to go, but there is a storm and the ocean waves are so high they will probably capsize the lifeboat. Do you try the lifeboat or stay on the sinking ship? You are five close friends who want to stay together.
4. You are in a mountain cabin with your family; sister or brother, father, mother, and your sister who is ill. Your father has a broken leg and must remain immobile. Your sister has all the symptoms of appendicitis and needs immediate medical attention. An avalanche is predicted, but you have a toboggan. What do you do? Who goes? Who stays, etc.?
5. You are stuck in an elevator with four other people. Each has an important reason to get out. What happens?

Another kind of improvisation is the *whole group* improvisation where everyone is involved. Everyone must take it seriously and stay in the character each chooses.

The group first decides where they are. For example, it could be a crowded airport, an emergency ward in a hospital, on an airplane, or a broken-down bus. When you create your own group improvisation, everyone must agree on the place.

Ask each person to decide who he or she is. What do they do for a living? What kind of person are they (happy, sad, etc.)? In other words, each person creates his own character.

Next decide what is happening. Have all flights been cancelled? Are you waiting to meet someone, when the announcement comes that there's been a crash? Has a catastrophe occurred to bring many people to the hospital? Is there a storm or a fogged-in airport that causes an immediate problem for the passengers? On the bus, has the driver lost his way? Did it slide over the side of a mountain or is the bus perched precariously on the edge of a cliff?

Get the idea? The next question is why? Why are each of the people there? What is their intent or purpose?

These are the same questions you can ask when you write your own play. But that's for the next chapter.

In the meantime, try improvisation.

Chapter 10

Writing Your Own Play

A play consists of plot, dialogue, and character. The plot is the story of what happens. Dialogue is what the characters say. And character is what makes them behave and speak the way they do.

Arthur Miller said, "The structure of a play is always the story of how the birds came home to roost."

George Abbott explained a play this way: "You get 'em up a tree. You throw stones at 'em. And you get 'em down."

There are thousands of plays to choose from. But suppose you want a play for a specific purpose or about a certain person? Maybe you need a play about an important historical figure for a school project.

In other words, you want to concentrate on that person or character for your play. But there are no published scripts about your important historical figure. What can you do? Can you write your own play? Where do you start?

Before you begin, try some exercises to get your imagination warmed up.

PLAYS FROM CHARACTERS

Go back to the last chapter on improvisation. Begin with those same techniques of improvisation. But, this time, concentrate on how different characters can change the situation or plot.

Begin with a simple situation for improvisation.

You have finished a large lunch in your favorite pizza parlor and you realize that you forgot your money. Explain your problem to:

1. An old friend who works there whom you see every day.
2. The old, sourpuss owner of the place who always says he hates kids.
3. A new waitress you've never seen before, on her first job.
4. A nervous, middle-aged waitress who's afraid she'll lose her job.

Do the improvisation four times with each character. See how different the improvisations will be. What are the feelings and emotions that occur? How does the dialogue differ from one character to another? Which of these character improvisations was the most dramatic? (Remember that drama is *conflict*.)

Try another improvisation. The characters will be more varied this time.

You are lost in an unfamiliar part of town. Ask directions from:

1. An elderly man who is hard of hearing.
2. A youngster of about seven or eight who's playing in front of his/her house.
3. A middle-aged woman who's frightened of you and thinks you're going to rob her.
4. A scary-looking man who frightens you.

Ask yourself the same questions you did after the last improvisation. Which of these improvisations was the most dramatic? Which would make the best story or drama?

Choose one of the improvisations to work on. Add another problem or element of conflict and try it. Let's take the first improvisation in the pizza parlor when you discover you have no money. For the character, try the old, sourpuss owner of the place who says he hates kids. Give him an additional problem. He wants to retire and sell the pizza parlor. He has no family and is free to move wherever he pleases.

"WHAT IF" TECHNIQUE

Ask yourself, "What if—"

What if the owner wants to retire and sell the pizza parlor? What if someone wants to buy the parlor for a suspicious reason? What if the kids will have no place to go?

Play the improvisation again with this new information and see what happens. For more drama, give the young person more elements of character.

What if he is broke and needs a job badly? What if he loves the old pizza parlor and feels like it's his second home? What if he's fond of the owner?

Play it again and see what happens. Add more "what

ifs" to increase the dramatic action. One thing that always helps drama is a sense of immediacy.

What if the potential buyer will be there any minute for the old man's answer? What if the young man has to get back to school or he'll be replaced on the basketball team if he's late one more time?

Get the idea? Take what worked in the improvisation and script it. (Write it out.) Don't expect perfection the first time. Every playwright knows his first draft is only the beginning.

Here's a sample of how the pizza parlor script could begin:

THE PIZZA PARLOR

CHARACTERS

Joey—about sixteen, friendly, nice kid.
Mr. S.—elderly owner of the pizza parlor, gruff exterior but really likes kids and is especially fond of Joey.

(THE SCENE IS SET AT THE COUNTER OF A PIZZA PARLOR. TWO CHARACTERS ARE THERE. ONE IS AN OLD MAN BEHIND THE COUNTER. THE OTHER IS A YOUNG MAN OF ABOUT SIXTEEN SEATED AT THE COUNTER.)

Mr. S: That's $1.58. (PUTS CHECK DOWN IN FRONT OF JOEY.)
Joey: (GOING THROUGH HIS POCKETS LOOKING FOR MONEY) Eh . . . er . . . hey. Mr. S, it looks like I've got a problem.
Mr. S: You and most of the world, Joey.
Joey: I mean—I-I've got an immediate problem.
Mr. S: What's your problem?
Joey: I must have left my wallet in my locker.

MR. S: Oh, you kids are all alike—always giving me trouble.

JOEY: Aw, come on, Mr. S. I never gave you any trouble. I'll pay you tomorrow, I promise. I have to go or I'll be late for practice.

MR. S: Tomorrow . . . tomorrow. It's always tomorrow. Well, I got news for you, kids. Maybe I won't be here tomorrow.

JOEY: What do you mean?

MR. S: I'm sellin' this dump. I'm sick and tired of it. I've had it with all you kids.

JOEY: You're kidding. (PAUSE) You wouldn't sell this place!

MR. S: Oh, yeah?—Just watch me. (LOOKS AT WATCH) As a matter of fact, you can watch me. Mr. Jaretti will be here in about ten minutes.

JOEY: Jake Jaretti?

MR. S: (SURPRISED) Yeah, how do you know?

JOEY: He sells dope to kids. That's how I know. He hangs around my brother's school.

MR. S: Nah! You're mistaken.

JOEY: No, I'm not, Mr. S. You can't sell the pizza parlor to him. You just can't.

MR. S: I already made the deal. All I have to do is sign . . .

JOEY: Don't do it!

Finish this one or start over again with your own improvisation and add a few of your "what if" complications.

You could continue the above scene by adding the other character. What if Jake Jaretti came in and heard Joey's accusation?

What if:

1. Mr. S. decided not to sell because of Joey's information.
2. Jake Jaretti vowed to get even with Joey.
3. Joey's brother worked for Jake Jaretti.

You can see more and more dramatic complications growing out of character.

PLAYS FROM STORIES

How about writing a play from a story? These are the easiest to do. You already have your characters, plot, and some of the dialogue.

Simply tell the story first. Then have your players make up their dialogue. Try it a few times. Let your players switch roles. Talk about which version was the most dramatic. Pick out the lines you thought moved the story forward. Improvise several times and then write out your script.

After your players have read it through, they will come up with suggestions for other lines or changes. Use the ideas that you think will work best. Try it again with the new ideas. Do it as many times as you want until the script meets with your approval or until you run out of ideas.

PLAYS FROM HISTORY

How about a play based on a historical event or character? When you do a play about an actual person, double check your facts. Make sure they are correct. Read enough about your character or event so you can visualize that person or persons in your own mind. See the people as individuals, as living, breathing, human beings (not just as historical figures).

Facts by themselves rarely make good drama. The use of a narrator is helpful to include important facts.

Let's say you've decided to do a play about George Washington, our first President. You have many choices of scenes to script and characters to use. For our purposes, let's take an event that is not quite as well known as some others. But the outcome of that event is seen by most of us every day, when we see a one-dollar bill. It's the portrait of George Washington. When and how was the original portrait painted and by whom?

Here are the historical facts:

1. The month was November 1793. The temporary capital of the country was in Germantown.

2. Gilbert Stuart was an eccentric given to all sorts of outlandish behavior.

3. Stuart had an athletic figure, sarcastic humor, and uncommon face. He had a good nature. He liked to tell jokes, and loved good food and drink.

4. Stuart had a daughter named Jane, who was devoted to him.

5. Artistically, Stuart's strength was in character study. Stuart observed Washington's face as being different from any he had ever observed.

6. The first portrait was called the Atheneum portrait and was painted by Gilbert Stuart in 1795, in Germantown outside of Philadelphia, Pa.

7. The so-called Marquis of Lansdown portrait (the full-length one) was painted in 1796.

8. There are mountains of historical facts about Washington, but the facts necessary for this scene must show that Washington was a man of great dignity and good breeding. He was smart and very much alive.

9. In 1796, when the full-length portrait was painted, Washington was sixty-four, his face was florid, and he had faulty dentures.

10. Washington never wanted to sit for a portrait. He did it as a favor to his wife.

These are the facts you will see dramatized in the following script. This is a scene from the play *Circle of Freedom*, which deals with this period in history. This script is more complicated than yours need be. It also uses a variety of theatrical devices. The characters of Samuel and Andrew function as narrators. The point is to see how the historical facts are used in an actual script.

CIRCLE OF FREEDOM*
by Dolly Beechman and Pat Sternberg

SCENE V—GILBERT STUART

<u>SAMUEL</u>

And so, during the month of November in 1793, Germantown was the seat of government of the United States. That month was as important as any in the whole eight years of President Washington's administration.

(ANDREW COMES DSR TO JOIN SAMUEL)

<u>ANDREW</u>

He came back to Germantown three more times. And we see the results of that visit almost every day.

<u>SAMUEL</u>

What do you mean?

<u>ANDREW</u>

Do you have a dollar bill in your pocket, Samuel?

<u>SAMUEL</u>

Yes, I think so, but why . . .

(REACHES IN POCKET AND TAKES OUT BILL)

<u>ANDREW</u>

(TAKING OUT BILL) Whose picture's on the dollar bill?

<u>SAMUEL</u>

(WITHOUT LOOKING AT BILL) George Washington. (SMILING) Everybody knows that.

<u>ANDREW</u>

Well, that portrait of George Washington was painted by Gilbert Stuart right here in Germantown.

*Copyright 1976

(LIGHTS UP ON SL AREA WHICH HAS NOW BECOME THE STUDIO OF GILBERT STUART. A SIGN INDICATES 5140 GERMANTOWN AVE.)

SAMUEL

Their first meeting must have been a pip.

ANDREW

Stuart was an eccentric given to all sorts of outlandish behavior, while the President was a man of great dignity.

(LIGHTS UP HALFWAY ON STUDIO AREA. WE SEE THE ACTION PANTOMIMED BUT NOT SPECIFICALLY AS ANDREW CONTINUES.)

(PRESIDENT WASHINGTON IS SEATED IN THE STUDIO AREA ON A CHAIR. HE SITS STIFFLY, WHILE STUART PRANCES AROUND TRYING TO MOVE THE CHAIR WITH THE PRESIDENT IN IT. STUART MOVES BACK AND FORTH TO HIS EASEL AND THE SUBJECT, TRYING TO GET EVERYTHING JUST RIGHT, BUT HE IS UNHAPPY WITH BOTH.)

ANDREW

The morning the President sat in his studio, Stuart exercised all his powers of charm and conversation to relax that set, inscrutable face . . . but, it was no use.

(PROJECTION OF ATHENEUM PORTRAIT. AS ANDREW CONTINUES, STUART PANTOMIMES A CONVERSATION WITH ANIMATION AND LAUGHTER. THE PRESIDENT DOES NOT REACT TO THIS. FINALLY, STUART LAUGHS RAUCOUSLY AND PRESIDENT WASHINGTON STANDS UP ANGRILY.)

WASHINGTON

(ANGRILY) Enough, Mr. Stuart. Save that kind of humor for the Blue Fox Tavern.

(HE EXITS SL.)

(ANDREW X UPSTAGE TO PROJECTION.)

ANDREW

The first portrait was not a success by Stuart's standards.

(STUART'S VOICE OVER, ANDREW POINTS TO PROJECTION OF PORTRAIT)

<u>Stuart (VOICE OVER)</u>

There were features in his face totally different from what I had observed in any other human being. The sockets of his eyes, for instance, were larger than what I had ever met with before, and the upper part of the nose broader. All his features were indicative of the strangest of passions. (THE PROJEC-TION ENLARGES) Yet, like Socrates, his judgment and self-command made him appear a man of a different cast in the eyes of the world. But the second time he sat for me, it was even worse. It was a disaster.

(LIGHTS UP IN STUDIO AREA. STUART IS MIXING HIS PAINTS. WASHINGTON ENTERS)

<u>WASHINGTON</u>

(TIGHT JAW) Good morning, Mr. Stuart. (HE WALKS TO THE SUBJECT CHAIR AND SITS.)

<u>STUART</u>

(EXCITED) Good heavens, sir. What is wrong with your mouth?

<u>WASHINGTON</u>

My new dentures are very ill-fitting, sir. I've ordered new ones, but in the meantime I must wear these.

<u>STUART</u>

But your whole face is distorted. How am I to paint you?

<u>WASHINGTON</u>

(QUIETLY) Shall we forget the whole thing, Mr. Stuart? (HE RISES)

<u>STUART</u>

(CALLING) No, no, of course not. I'll think of something.

(HE SEATS THE PRESIDENT.)
(HE PICKS UP APPLE AND BEGINS TO CUT IT.)
(X TO WASHINGTON) Perhaps if we stuff your cheeks with bits of apple . . . (CUTTING APPLE)
(WASHINGTON STANDS UP AND ASSUMES THE STANCE OF THE LANSDOWN PORTRAIT.)

<u>STUART</u>

If that doesn't work, we'll try stuffing your cheeks with cotton wadding.

WASHINGTON

(HOLDING HIS HAND UP TO STOP HIM) Cotton wadding, if you please, Mr. Stuart.

(PROJECTION OF LANSDOWN PORTRAIT)

ANDREW

It was cotton wadding that they finally settled on, and the Lansdown portrait was completed in 1796. Once again, Stuart was unhappy with the results.

(LIGHTS UP ON STUDIO AREA. STUART IS LOOKING AT HIS EASEL WHILE PROJECTION IS STILL UP.)

STUART

Washington's shoulders are too high and narrow. His hands and feet are remarkably large. He has an ungainly stance. (HIS ANNOYANCE RISING) And the face, those ill-fitting teeth— even with the cotton—give his face a set expression. I must try again.

(LIGHTS FADE OUT)

ANDREW

Stuart got his chance to try again in August 1796, when the First Lady, Martha Washington, asked Stuart to paint the family portraits.

(LIGHTS UP IN THE STUDIO AREA. STUART IS PREPARING HIS PAINTS AT THE EASEL. THERE IS A KNOCK AT THE DOOR. JANE ENTERS WITH A WOOL SKEIN AROUND HER FINGERS. SHE USHERS IN THE PRESIDENT, WHO NODS HIS THANKS AND TAKES HIS SEAT. STUART NOTICES THE PRESIDENT'S PLEASANT SMILE TO JANE.)

STUART

(SEIZING AN IDEA, HE HALTS JANE'S EXIT.) Perhaps you'll stay and chat with the President, Jane—(WHISPERING TO HER)—to keep his face relaxed.

(WASHINGTON ASSUMES A RIGID POSE IN THE CHAIR.)

JANE

But Father, I must wind the wool.

STUART

(WHISPERING TO JANE) Look at that pose! That man is made of granite. (HE THROWS UP HIS HANDS)

WASHINGTON

(STIFFLY) Ready, Mr. Stuart.

JANE

(WHISPERING TO HER FATHER) I wouldn't know what to talk about, Father.

STUART

Talk about apple trees or horse chestnuts . . . anything. You never have any trouble prattling on when I want it quiet.

JANE

(GIGGLING) Oh, Father.
(SHE X TO WASHINGTON AND BEGINS TO SPEAK SELF-CONSCIOUSLY) And . . . how, eh . . . how is the First Lady, Mr. President?

WASHINGTON

(NOTICING HER DIFFICULTY WITH THE WOOL IN HER HANDS.) Here, let me help you with that.

(HE TAKES THE WOOL FROM HER HANDS AND PUTS IT ON HIS, AND SHE BEGINS TO WIND THE BALL OF WOOL.)

That's a fine mare tethered outside. I'd say it's just about the right size for a young lady.

JANE

Oh, it is, sir. She's mine. And a finer mare you couldn't find in all of Germantown and maybe the world.

WASHINGTON

Oh, you think so. Well, you'll just have to see some of my mares on my plantation on the Potomac. . . .

(FADE OUT)
(PROJECTION OF ATHENEUM PORTRAIT, THE ONE ON THE DOLLAR BILL)

ANDREW

At last, here was a portrait Stuart could delight in. On the whole, it was Stuart's best rapport with the President.

WASHINGTON

(X TO LOOK OVER STUART'S SHOULDER) I shall be perfectly satisfied with copies from your hand, Mr. Stuart.

(HE SHAKES HANDS WITH STUART, BOWS TO JANE AND EXITS.)

ANDREW

(XDSC) Stuart visualized the fortune he could make producing copies.
(CALLING OFFSTAGE) Oh, Jane . . . Tell us, how long did it take your father to paint one of those copies?

JANE

(ENTERS SL AND X TO HIM) Not long. Father could dash off a copy in about two hours. He kept the unfinished portrait by him for the rest of his life. (SHE LAUGHS) Father called those canvases his "hundred-dollar bills."

(BLACKOUT)
(DOLLAR BILL PROJECTION)

SAMUEL

Gilbert Stuart was often imitated but never surpassed. And it all happened in Germantown, the studio where Gilbert Stuart painted the portrait that went on our dollar bills—first in 1889.

(FADE OUT)
(CURTAIN)

A lot more research goes into a historical play than just the facts mentioned. But this gives you an idea of how history can be brought to life through drama.

PLAYS FROM HISTORICAL CHARACTERS

When you deal with one person in history, rather than an event, you face a different problem. You must capture the essence of that person as a human being. His or her character is what shaped the historical event.

Here's an example of a play based on a character, Sojourner Truth. She was an unusual woman and far ahead of her time. Look at the facts. See how they are used in this scene from the play *Sojourner,* by Dolly Beechman and Pat Sternberg.

Historical facts used in the scene are:

1. Sojourner Truth was a slave from the state of New York. (New York set slaves free in 1827, much earlier than other states.)
2. Sojourner was very religious and felt she spoke directly to God.
3. She had a magnificent singing voice and could hold the attention of large crowds.
4. She traveled across the country, singing and preaching. (She was a sojourner.)
5. She was a large woman who worked as hard as any man.
6. Sojourner attended a women's rights convention in Akron, Ohio.
7. The feminist movement opposed slavery and fought for all human rights.
8. Mrs. Francis D. Gage presided at the meeting.
9. Ministers from the Methodist, Baptist, Episcopal, Presbyterian, and Universalist churches were present.
10. This was the convention where Sojourner made her famous "Ain't I a woman" speech.

Pick out each of the specific facts as you come across them in the scene. That will show you how the historical incidents are used dramatically.

SOJOURNER*

by Dolly Beechman and Pat Sternberg

(THE SCENE TAKES PLACE IN A LARGE MEETING HALL. THE CLERGYMEN ARE IN THE AUDIENCE AND COME FORWARD WHEN THEY SPEAK. THERE IS NOISE FROM THE PROTESTING CROWD.)

*Copyright 1978

<u>Mrs. Gage</u>

(SHE IS ONSTAGE AT THE PODIUM. SHE BANGS GAVEL.)

Order, order. I will have order at this meeting. The chair recognizes our guests, the ministers from the Methodist, Baptist, Episcopal, Presbyterian, and Universalist churches. Welcome, gentlemen.

<u>Voice #1</u>

Let them speak.

(CROWD NOISES)

<u>Mrs. Gage</u>

Reverend Goodbody, you have the floor.

<u>Man #1</u>

Of course, the Lord intended man to have superior rights and privileges. Did the Lord not make his intellect superior to that of a woman?

(APPLAUSE AND CHEERS, WHISTLES, ETC.)

<u>Man #2</u>

(TAKING UP THE WORD) Wasn't Christ a man? Wouldn't God at that time have given some token of his divine wish to have women equal—if he had wanted it that way?

<u>Man #1</u>

(SHAKING HIS FINGER) According to the Bible, it was not man but woman who sinned by accepting the apple from the serpent. Isn't that proof of God's wish to make her inferior?

<u>Man #2</u>

Women! Beware of selling your birthright of consideration for a mess of equality pottage.

<u>Man #3</u>

What man would help another man into a carriage or over a ditch? These courtesies are the rights and privileges of women!

(SOJOURNER TRUTH STANDS AND WAITS TO BE RECOGNIZED. A HUSH FALLS OVER THE CROWD.)

<u>Mrs. Gage</u>

The chair recognizes Sojourner Truth.

(AUDIENCE QUIETS DOWN)

SOJOURNER

Well, children, where there is so much racket, there must be
something out of kilter. I think between the colored folks of
the South and the women of the North—all talkin' about
rights—the white men will be in a pretty fix soon.

VOICE #1

Who do you think you are, Joan of Arc?

SOJOURNER

That man over there. (SHE POINTS AT ONE OF THE MIN-
ISTERS) He says women need to be helped into carriages and
lifted over ditches and to have the best everywhere. (SHE
SMILES AND SHAKES HER HEAD NEGATIVELY) Nobody
ever helps me into carriages, over mud puddles, or gets me any
best places. Ain't I a woman? Look at me. (SHE ROLLS UP
HER SLEEVE TO DISPLAY HER MUSCULAR ARM AND
HOLDS IT UP HIGH) Look at my arm. I have ploughed, and
I have planted. And I have gathered into barns. And no man
could head me. And, ain't I a woman? I could work as much
and eat as much as any man . . . when I could get it. And bear
the lash as well. (HER VOICE RISING) And, ain't I a woman?
I have borne children and none but Jesus heard me. And, ain't
I a woman? (SHE LOOKS OVER AT THE MINISTER AND
POINTS TO HIM) He talks about this thing in the head. (SHE
HESITATES AND LOOKS TO THE WOMAN NEAREST
HER) What's that they call it?

WOMAN #2

(WHISPERS) Intellect.

SOJOURNER

That's it, honey. (SHE NODS APPROVINGLY AND TURNS
HER ATTENTION BACK TO THE AUDIENCE) What's that
got to do with women's rights or colored folks' rights? If my
cup won't hold but a pint, and yours holds a quart, wouldn't
you be mean not to let me have my little measure?

WOMAN #2

Why, that's right.

(SHE QUICKLY PUTS HER HAND OVER HER MOUTH
AS IF SURPRISED BY HER OUTBURST.)

<u>SOJOURNER</u>
(POINTING TO ANOTHER) That little man in black there.
He says women can't have as much rights as men, 'cause Christ
wasn't a woman. (HER ARMS OUTSTRETCHED) Where did
Christ come from? (SHE LOOKS DIRECTLY AT HIM) From
God and a woman. Man had nothing to do with him.
(THERE IS AN AUDIBLE GASP IN THE AUDIENCE. SO-
JOURNER SMILES, KNOWING SHE HAS MADE HER
POINT. NOW SHE TURNS HER ATTENTION BACK TO
THE WOMEN IN THE AUDIENCE.)

<u>SOJOURNER</u>
If the first woman God ever made was strong enough to turn
the world upside down all alone, these women together ought
to be able to turn it back and get it right side up again. And
now that they are asking to do it, the men better let 'em. And
now, old Sojourner has nothing more to say.
(SHE STOOPS OVER AND PICKS UP HER BONNET.)
Obliged to you for hearing me.
(SHE WALKS OFF AND THE WHOLE AUDIENCE AP-
PLAUDS.)

Could you pick out the ten facts from the list which
were dramatized in the play? How else could they be
done? Can you think of another scene where these facts
could be used?

PLAYS FROM CURRENT ISSUES OR PROBLEMS

One of the best ways to write a play is to write about
something you know and care about or is of great interest
to you. What are some current issues that affect you either
in your community, school, or home? What are some of
your problems or those of your friends? Would any of
these things make a good play?

Here's where a group effort can help. Toss around ideas for improvisation on a school problem, a family problem, a problem with a boyfriend or girlfriend. What's going on in the world that could make a difference in your life?

Plays don't have to be serious. Neil Simon, the well-known playwright, brings laughter to millions of people through his comedies. What's funny to you? What are some funny situations you or your friends have experienced? Real comedy grows out of situations. What funny situation happened to you or to others?

Don't expect to write a play like Neil Simon when you begin. He had to begin somewhere. So can you.

Writing a play is hard work. It is also an exciting adventure. Try it! It might be just the thing for your group. You can always change your mind and go back to a scripted play if it doesn't work out. You will learn an appreciation for drama and the playwright when you try it for yourself. You will realize more than ever: "The play's the thing."

Chapter **11**

Break a Leg!

TIPS ON HOW TO MAKE YOUR OWN GOOD LUCK

To collaborate means to work together. Putting on a play calls for the collaboration of many different people with many different talents. Teamwork is vital in play production. Putting on a play demands the same kind of physical effort, concentration, and practice that any team sport does.

At the same time, one person must be in charge of the production. That person (usually the director) must see that no single element of the production overshadows the rest.

There's no place for a star either onstage or backstage in amateur theater. Everyone must work together to produce the best possible creative effort. The old saying: "A chain is as strong as its weakest link" could easily refer to play production.

Remember how important every job is. Go back to Chapters 2 and 3 and review the responsibilities of each person working on the production. Make sure everyone in the play understands his or her job. The more carefully you organize the work and plan your rehearsal period, the more successful your production will be.

Let's review what each person on the production staff does.

DIRECTOR—He or she casts the play, blocks and conducts rehearsals. He or she approves all production designs and sees that those designs are put into practice.

ASSISTANT DIRECTOR—(Optional) He or she helps the director in any area needed, frequently takes over administrative details.

STAGE MANAGER—He or she is the director's right hand, writes down all the blocking and cues in the stage manager's book (prompt book). He or she runs the show during performance.

TECHNICAL DIRECTOR—He or she is in charge of building the set, may function as the designer and frequently does the lights also.

FRONT OF HOUSE—This category includes all the people who do publicity, box office, program, ushers, etc.

PRODUCTION CREWS—One person should be in charge of the following areas: props, lights, costumes, make-up, and sound.

Make yourself a sign that says "PLAN AHEAD" and place it someplace where you will see it every day. It is an important thing to remember. Don't make the mistake of waiting until the last minute to find a necessary prop. And don't think that problems will work themselves out. Nothing just happens. Somebody makes it happen.

It is vital to have props and furniture in plenty of time so that actors can rehearse with them. The more rehearsals an actor has with the actual items he will use, the more natural his actions will be onstage.

Make sure all your technical effects—sound, lights,

etc.—are worked out exactly the way the director wants them. Spend as much time as necessary to work out all the cues and effects.

Never assume that when the time comes, it will be all right. There's only one way to make sure your technical effects will be right. Rehearse them again and again until they are perfect. Through all this, the director must maintain a relaxed atmosphere, as well as a firm hand.

If tempers and emotions flare up among your players, stop. Try something to relax or revitalize everyone. Ask

An actor learns many different things during the course of a play production.

your cast to try the play in a different style or do it as a comic opera. Put on some music and have them dance the mood of their character. Have your actors exchange parts. Sometimes it is more important to relax the atmosphere than to create perfection for the moment. This is time well spent and will pay off in the long run. When you go back to the regular rehearsal, your players will be refreshed.

Invite people to watch the later stages of rehearsal. One director has a preview after his final dress rehearsal and invites some special group to see the performance. This way he gets at least two full dress rehearsals at performance level.

REHEARSAL SCHEDULES

There is no magic number of rehearsals that will ensure a polished performance. Each type of play has its individual requirements. The longer and more complicated the show, the more rehearsal it takes.

Most directors follow the same general pattern for rehearsal procedure. The first rehearsal is usually a read through and discussion of characterization, motivation, meaning of the play, etc. Some directors have two or three read throughs.

Directors prefer blocking at the next session. They block the acts in their order in the play. After blocking is completed, the director sets a deadline for knowing lines.

Generally speaking, the last week is set for polishing. Then comes the technical and dress rehearsals and possibly a preview before the opening.

"I must admit, I'm superstitious about the theater. Everyone knows that whistling in a dressing room is bad luck," a university theater director confided. "The other thing I'm superstitious about is the number of rehearsals I have for a play. My lucky number is twenty-one. I always have twenty-one rehearsals before opening. Anything less than that, something always goes wrong. And any more—my actors go stale."

SPECIFIC SCHEDULES

Take a look at the following schedules, which were actually used for the designated productions.

The first one is a rehearsal schedule for a melodrama that was performed by the Teen Repertory Theatre in Riverdale, New York, directed by Pat Sternberg.

REHEARSAL SCHEDULE

EGAD, WHAT A CAD! by Anita Bell

Date	Time	Work
Feb. 1 - Mon.	3–5	Read through
Feb. 3 - Wed.	3–5	Read through
Feb. 6 - Sat.	1–5	Block Scene I
Feb. 8 - Mon.	3–5	Block Scene 2
Feb. 10 - Wed.	3–5	Run Act II
Feb. 13 - Sat.	1–5	Run Act I and II
Feb. 15 - Mon.	3–5	Run Act I
Feb. 17 - Wed.	3–5	Run Act II
Feb. 20 - Sat.	1–5	Scene 1 - lines
Feb. 22 - Mon.	3–5	Scene 2 - lines
Feb. 24 - Wed.	3–5	Scene 1 and 2
Feb. 25 - Thurs.	3–5	Run Act I, II
Feb. 27 - Sat.	1–5	Run through (costumes)
Feb. 28 - Sun.	1–finish	Tech
March 1 - Mon.	7–10	Run through (make-up)
March 2 - Tues.	7–10	Run through
March 3 - Wed.	7–10	Dress
March 4 - Thurs.	7	Preview
March 5–6 - Fri. & Sat.	7	Performance

The following rehearsal schedule was a musical for children's theater. It took an hour to perform. It was done by the Riverdale Children's Theatre with youngsters (ages seven through fourteen) playing the parts.

REHEARSAL SCHEDULE
THE CURIOUS ADVENTURE by Pat Sternberg

Date	Work	Time
Nov. 17	Saturday .. Act I & II walk through	10–1
Nov. 26	Monday . . . . Second walk through	3:30–5
Dec. 1	Saturday . . Act I walk through	10–1
Dec. 3	Monday . . . Act II walk through	3:30–5
Dec. 4	Tuesday . . . Act III walk through	3:30–5
Dec. 7	Friday . . . . Act I lines	3:30–5
Dec. 8	Saturday . . Act I lines perfect—songs	10–1
Dec. 15	Saturday . . Act II lines—Act II songs	10–1
Jan. 5	Saturday . . Act II lines perfect	10–1
Jan. 12	Saturday . . Act I & II lines	10–1
Jan. 19	Saturday . . Act III lines	3:30–5
Jan. 21	Monday . . . . Act III lines perfect	3:30–5
Jan. 22	Tuesday . . . Act III lines	3:30–5
Jan. 26	Saturday . . Trouble act	10–1
Jan. 28	Monday . . . . Trouble act	3:30–5
Jan. 29	Tuesday . . . Act III (with songs)	3:30–5
Feb. 2	Saturday . . Trouble spots	10–1
Feb. 4	Monday . . . . Trouble spots	3:30–5
Feb. 5	Tuesday . . . Complete run through	3:30–5
Feb. 13	Wednesday . Complete run through with costumes & set	3:30–5
Feb. 15	Friday . . . . Dress rehearsal	3:30
Feb. 16	Saturday . . Performance	3:30

This was a rehearsal schedule for a full-length straight play with a large cast.

REHEARSAL SCHEDULE
THE SCHOLARSHIP FUND by Pat Sternberg

7 P.M. in 9B unless otherwise noted

March 16	Tues.	Tryouts
March 17	Wed.	
March 18	Thurs.	Read through
March 22	Mon.	Crew only
March 23	Tues.	Read through Act I
March 24	Wed.	Read through Act II
March 25	Thurs.	Read through Acts I, II
March 30	Tues.	Block Act I, 1
March 31	Wed.	Block Act I, 2, 3
April 1	Thurs.	Block Act II, 1, 2
April 6	Tues.	Block Act II, 3,4
April 7	Wed.	Act I - Lines
April 8	Thurs.	Act I
April 12	Mon.	Act I - Lines
April 13	Tues.	Act II - Lines
April 15	Thurs.	Act II - Lines
April 17	Sat. (10 A.M.)	Run through
April 19	Mon.	Act I
April 20	Tues.	Act II
April 21	Wed.	Act I, II
April 22	Thurs.	Act I, II
April 23	Fri.	Trouble spots
April 24	Sat. (10 A.M.)	Tech.
		Make-up, Dress &
April 25	Sun. (10 A.M.)	Tech.
April 26	Mon.	Dress
April 27	Tues.	Dress
April 28	Wed.	Preview
April 29	Thurs. (5:30 P.M.)	Rehearsal
April 30 }	Fri.	Performance
May 1 }	Sat.	
May 5	Wed.	Pick-up Rehearsal
May 7 }	Fri.	Performance
May 8 }	Sat.	

The following rehearsal schedule was for a theater for youth production at Hunter College. This was an unusually long play for that type. It ran almost an hour and a half and had some music, several songs, and simple dances.

REHEARSAL SCHEDULE

THE BEEPLE by Alan Cullen

DIRECTOR: Pat Sternberg
STG. MGR: Irena Nicolai

Date	Day	Time	Work
March 2	Mon.	2–4	Block Act I to pg. 21
March 4	Wed.	3–6	Block Act I pg. 22–35
March 9	Mon.	2–4	Run Act I
March 11	Wed.	3–6	Block Act II - 1, 2, 4
March 16	Mon.	2–4	Block Act II - 3, 5
March 18	Wed.	3–6	Run Act II
March 23	Mon.	2–4	Block Act III - 1, 2, 3
March 25	Wed.	3–6	Block Act III - 4, 5
			Run Act III
March 30	Mon.	2–4	T.B.A.*
April 1	Wed.	3–6	Run Acts I & II
April 6	Mon.	2–4	Run Act III
April 9	Wed.	3–6	Act I (lines)

(Rehearsals in Little Theatre from now on)

April 13	Mon.	2–5	Act II (lines)
April 15	Wed.	3–6	Acts II, III (lines)
April 17	Fri.	T.B.A.	T.B.A.

Spring Break T.B.A.

April 27	Mon.	2–5	Act I
April 28	Tues.	7:30	Acts II & III
April 29	Wed.	3–6	Run through
April 30	Thurs.	7–10	T.B.A.
May 1	Fri.	T.B.A.	T.B.A.
May 2	Sat.	10–6	Tech.
May 3	Sun.	10–6	Dress (make-up)
May 4	Mon.	3–6	Dress
May 5	Tues.	6	Preview

*T.B.A. means *to be announced*

COPING WITH THE UNEXPECTED

Some theater directors proceed under the assumption: "If anything can go wrong, it will." Sooner or later, every actor and/or director must cope with the unexpected. Some problems occur more frequently than others.

What do you do when another actor is late for an entrance?

"I ad-lib and try to say the cue, but in a way the audience won't know I'm repeating it," advised one veteran actress.

"If it doesn't go against the script, I yell for him," said another. "And if that doesn't work, I invent a lot of stage business—pour a drink, check the tables for dust, fluff the cushions on the couch—that kind of stuff."

"I go out and get him," said another actor.

"What bothers me the most," admitted a young actor, "is when the other actor gives you the wrong cue. He may have skipped several pages in the script, so you have to get him back where he's supposed to be without making it obvious to the audience. But you have to make him realize what you're doing. I say things like 'Aren't you getting ahead of yourself Charlie? Don't you mean . . .' or 'as I said before.' "

"That's happened to me more than once!" an actress responded. "I always look the character right in the eye and say, 'You don't mean that, do you . . .' and then I give him a look."

Most actors agree that there's something even worse than a late entrance or wrong cue. That's when the other actor comes on too soon. What do you do then?

"That is absolutely the hardest thing to deal with," a young actress lamented. "That happened to me once. It was so dumb. I wasn't supposed to know he was there. I squinted my eyes and said something about my contact lens slipping and I couldn't see a thing. He got the idea and left quickly."

Actors learn to deal with these kinds of situations by ad-libbing. But there are times when even the ad-lib won't work. Most amateur and school plays don't have understudies. What happens when one of your players is sick and cannot be in the play? What about the old saying: "The show must go on!" Short of canceling the performance, what can you do?

A community theater director said, "I did a children's theater production of *The Curious Adventure* a few years ago. One of the main characters, the Prime Minister, got sick the day of the show. He absolutely couldn't go on. One of the kids on the prop crew was familiar with the play but couldn't learn the lines in such a short time. We made a fancy ledger book—a great big one—for the actor to carry and continually check his accounts. Of course, the script was inside. It worked fine. The show went on as scheduled."

"I did something like that once," said an actress. "I had to replace another actress. I tried to learn the lines overnight, but I couldn't. So I wrote them in chalk on the floor of the stage, and I pasted part of the script on the desk and part on the couch and the rest on a table. That way I could move around, getting some of the blocking right anyway. At least I didn't stay in one place. The best part of it was—nobody noticed what I was doing."

One of the hardest things to cope with onstage is the "break" (when you come out of character). Something will strike you so funny that no matter what you do, you have to laugh. And, although you know you must concentrate, the laugh or smile takes over. Is there any way to handle that? There are some tricks that actors use when this happens. The simplest solution, of course, is to turn upstage, away from the audience so they don't see your face.

"Use it, if you can," advised another actor. "If there's any way you can, use it as the character would. Say something like 'Oh, I'm sorry I laughed, but what you just did reminded me of my crazy Uncle Harry. He was always doing the funniest things.' "

"I stick my thumbnail in my finger so hard it hurts. The pain brings back my concentration," admitted another young player. "If that doesn't work, I bite the corner of my cheek. It hurts but it works."

There are all kinds of tricks for coping with the unexpected. One of the most exciting elements of live theater is dealing with whatever occurs here and now. How about missing props or sound effects? Can those kinds of problems ever be solved? Sometimes yes and sometimes no. But you should always try something.

"I remember one time we took our play to another school and we forgot the blanks for the pistol. There was no place to get any, so we had to improvise. Frankly, I was stumped," a young director admitted. "But thank goodness one of the actors came up with an idea for the sound. He banged two pieces of two-by-fours together. It wasn't a perfect sound, but it passed."

"Last week we lost the clerical collar for our priest in the play, but we improvised that one pretty fast. We took a piece of white paper, folded it, and pinned it in place," a young actor offered.

"If the missing prop is small enough, you can pantomime it. Or you can mask the missing object. Put your hand or body in front of it and act as if it's there. The audience will believe it as long as you seem to," a director suggested.

"Experience is the best teacher," is an old adage. Everyone learns to deal with the unexpected in the theater. That is part of the excitement and appeal of working onstage.

What you can do, however, is to make sure all the elements you can control are as prepared and ready as possible.

How can you tell if you're ready for opening night. You're ready if your answers to the following questions are "Yes."

- Do all the actors know their lines?
- Do you have all your props?
- Is the set ready and functional?
- Are all the costumes fitted and ready? (Are the actors comfortable in them?)
- Are all your sound cues coming at exactly the right time?
- Are all your light cues running smoothly and on time?
- Does the make-up look natural and convincing?
- Is the front of house ready for business? (Tickets, box-office, ushers, etc.?)
- Are the programs ready?
- Do you have an audience? (Sell tickets or give them away beforehand if possible. Invite all your friends and family.)

CONCLUSION

Theater people speak of getting "the bug." It can be the "acting bug" or the general "theater bug." But whichever bug it is, it can affect you for your entire lifetime. Once you've experienced the excitement and joy of an opening night, you'll want to experience it again and again. Some of us never get "the bug" out of our system, and many of us never want to.

As an avocation, the theater can offer a lifetime of joy, adventure, excitement, and understanding. You will learn about yourself, other people, and your environment. You will learn about other times, both in the past and predictions for the future. You will learn about other cultures and ways of thinking. You will experience laughter, tears, and a variety of emotions. Where else can you live a hundred different lives? There's nothing quite like it. Once you begin a love affair with the theater, it will last forever.

Remember, theater people are superstitious. They never say "good luck." They say "break a leg!"

Glossary of Theater Terms

Ad-lib—To make up dialogue on the spot to cover a forgotten or late cue.

Arena theater (theater-in-the-round)—The audience is seated on all four sides of the acting area.

Backstage—The area unseen by the audience behind the stage, off to the side, or the dressing room area.

Breakaway (costume or prop)—An object that is already prepared to break or split easily.

Blocking—The movement of the actors onstage.

Business (stage business)—What an actor does on stage (e.g., eat a piece of candy, pick up a box, etc.).

Choreographer—The dance director who creates the dances and movement patterns in a musical.

Classroom play—A play given for the benefit of the members of a class with everyone participating in some way with little or no production elements.

Conflict—The problem or struggle of the characters which leads to the climax of a play.

Crew—The backstage part of the team needed to put on a production.

Cue—The line, business, movement, or effect which signals the next action or speech.

Curtain—The rise of the curtain signals the beginning and the fall signals the end of a scene, act, or the play.

Director—The person responsible for the overall production. He or she blocks the show, rehearses the actors, and coordinates all other elements.

Downstage—The front of the stage closest to the audience.

Ensemble—A group which is dependent on several or all players rather than one.

Exit—An actor *exits* when he leaves the stage. It is also the physical place where he leaves.

First read through—The reading of the entire script for the first time by the actors with the director.

Flat—A single piece of lightweight scenery to suggest a wall or part of the boundary that makes up the set.

Flyer—A hand bill to advertise the play usually smaller than a poster.

Front of house—The auditorium or area of the theater where the audience gathers.

Gel—A thin sheet of colored plastic material placed over a light to reflect a color onto the stage.

Improvisation—Spontaneous dialogue and actions made up on the spot.

Notes—Suggestions for improvement given to the cast and crew by the director.

Offstage—The area of the stage or behind it which is not in view of the audience.

Onstage—The area of the stage in view of the audience.

Pantomime—Action without words.

Paper the house—Give away free tickets to ensure an audience.

Plot—The arrangement of incidents which make up the story of the play.

Prompt—To give a line or cue in case an actor forgets.

Prompt book (stage manager's book)—The script with blocking, business, and all cues (light, sound, etc.) written in.

Proscenium—The frame of the stage opening which separates the audience from the playing area.

Readers' theater—Plays read for an audience with little or no staging.

Rehearsal—The practice and repetition of a play by the actors guided by the director to prepare for a performance.

Royalty—The money paid to a play publisher or the author for the right to do the play.

Script—The written version of a play which includes dialogue and actions.

Set—The scenery which creates the environment for the entire play.

Set piece—A part of the scenery, which can stand alone to suggest part or all of the environment.

Stage left—The left side of the stage from an actor's point of view as he faces the audience.

Stage right—The right side of the stage from an actor's point of view as he faces the audience.

Technical—The non-acting elements of the production (lights, sound, etc.).

Upstage—The area farthest away from the audience toward the back or rear.

Voice over—The projected voice of an actor heard without being seen.

Sources of Materials

PLAYS

I.E. Clark, Inc.
St. John's Road
Dept. CT
Schulenburg, TX 78956

Performance Publishing Co.
978 North McLean Blvd.
Elgin, IL 60120

Players Press, Inc.
P.O. Box 1132
Studio City, CA 91604

The Coach House Press
53 W. Jackson Blvd.
Chicago, IL 60604

Already listed in text:

Samuel French, Inc.
Dramatists Play Service
Tams-Witmark Music
   Library, Inc.

David McKay
750 Third Ave.
New York, NY 10017

Pioneer Drama Service
P.O. Box 22555
Denver, CO 80222

Modern Theatre for Youth
2366 Grandview Terrace
Manhattan, KS 66502

Reader's Theater Script
   Service
P.O. Box 178333
San Diego, CA 92117

New Plays, Inc.
Anchorage Press
Plays, Inc.
Scholastic Magazines, Inc.

GENERAL THEATRICAL SUPPLIES

(The following companies offer a full line of all theatrical supplies including lights, costumes, make-up, props, etc.)

Rubies Costume Co., Inc.
One Rubie Plaza
Richmond Hill, NY 11418

American Scenic
P.O. Box 283
11 Andrews St.
Greenville, SC 29602

151

Norcostco-Atlanta Costume
2089 Monroe Drive N.E.
Atlanta, GA 30324

Norcostco-California
    Costume
2101 W. Garvey No.
West Covina, CA 91790

Norcostco-Texas Costume
2125 North Harwood St.
Dallas, TX 75201

Norcostco-Northwestern
    Costume
3203 No. Highway 100
Minneapolis, MN 55422

Companies specializing in lights, sound, rigging, etc.

Olesen
1535 Ivar Ave.
Hollywood, CA 90028

McManus Enterprises
111 Union Ave.
Bala Cynwood, PA 19004

Times Square Theatrical
    and Studio Supply Corp.
318 West 47th St.
New York, NY 10036

Lighting

Production Arts
636 Eleventh Ave.
New York, NY 10011

Four Star Lighting
585 Gerard Ave.
Bronx, NY 10045

Costumes

Broadway Costumes, Inc.
932 West Washington Blvd.
Chicago, IL 60607

Krause Costume Co.
2439 Superior Ave.
Cleveland, OH 44114

Dazians, Inc.
2014 Commerce St.
Dallas, TX 75201

(Specializing in rentals)

Eves Costume Co., Inc.
423 West 55th St.
New York, NY 10036

Brooks-Van Horn Costume
    Co.
117 West 17th St.
New York, NY 10011

Make-up

Stein's Theatrical Make-up
M. Stein Cosmetic Co.
430 Broome St.
New York, NY 10013

Bob Kelly Cosmetics, Inc.
151 West 46th St.
New York, NY 10036

Ben Nye Co., Inc.
11571 Santa Monica Blvd.
Los Angeles, CA 90025

Tickets

ATS Ticket Service
375 North Broadway
Jericho, NY 11730

Ticket Craft
1925 Bellmore Ave.
Bellmore, NY 11710

Selected Bibliography

Davis, Jed and Mary Ann Hatkins. *Children's Theatre*. New York: Harper & Row, Inc., 1981.

Dezseran, Louis John. *The Student Actor's Handbook*. Palo Alto, Calif.: Mayfield Publishing Co., 1975.

Donahue, John Clark and Linda Walsh Jenkins. *Five Plays from the Children's Theatre Company of Minneapolis*. Minneapolis: Univ. of Minnesota Press, 1975.

Hodgson, John. *Improvisation*. London: Methune and Co., Ltd., 1966.

MAGAZINES OF INTEREST

Plays, Inc.
8 Arlington St.
Boston, MA 02116

Theatre Crafts
33 East Minor St.
Emmaus, PA 18049

155

INDEX

157

About the Author

Playwright, actress, and director, Patricia Sternberg is a professor of Theatre & Film at Hunter College in New York City. She directs the MADHATTERS, a group of college students who perform in plays for young people.

She has had over twenty plays published and/or produced. Two of her plays, both written with Dolly Beechman, *Treaty Never Broken* and *Sojourner* are running currently.

Her career as an actress began at the age of eleven with the role of the witch in *Snow White and the Seven Dwarfs*. She has been involved in some area of the theater ever since.

Other principal characters in the author's life are Richard (husband), David (son), and Ruth and Anne (daughters).